INDIA-PAKISTAN NEGOTIATIONS
IS PAST STILL PROLOGUE?

INDIA-PAKISTAN NEGOTIATIONS

Also in the *Perspectives Series*

Manufacturing Human Bombs: The Making of Palestinian Suicide Bombers

Perspectives on Pacifism: Christian, Jewish, and Muslim Views on Nonviolence and International Conflict

Islamic Activism and U.S. Foreign Policy

Power Sharing and International Mediation in Ethnic Conflicts

Islam and Democracy

Religious Perspectives on War

Conflict Resolution in the Middle East

India-Pakistan Negotiations

Is Past Still Prologue?

Dennis Kux

UNITED STATES INSTITUTE OF PEACE PRESS
Washington, DC

UNITED STATES INSTITUTE OF PEACE
1200 17th Street NW, Suite 200
Washington, DC 20036-3011

www.usip.org

First edition 2006

Printed in the United States of America

Library of Congress Cataloging-in-Publication Data

Kux, Dennis, 1931–
  India-Pakistan negotiations : is past still prologue? / Dennis Kux.
    p. cm.
  Includes bibliographical references.
  ISBN-13: 978-1-929223-87-9 (pbk. : alk. paper)
  ISBN-10: 1-929223-87-0 (pbk. : alk. paper)
  1. India--Foreign relations--Pakistan. 2. Pakistan--Foreign relations--India. I. Title.

DS450.P18K89 2006
327.5405491–dc22

                                                      2006001052

CONTENTS

FOREWORD

After more than fifty years of independence, India and Pakistan confront many of the same intractable issues that the British left for these new countries to resolve. Kashmir remains to be one of many legacies of their distrust and suspicion. Their joint enmity has led them into three wars, the Kargil Crisis of 1999, and several near conflicts.

Over the past two years, India and Pakistan have been able to begin and sustain a comprehensive negotiating process oriented toward normalizing their troubled bilateral relations, a process known as the "composite dialogue." While the tragic October 2005 earthquake in Pakistan elicited brief bilateral cooperation related to disbursing humanitarian relief, it also rekindled mistrust among Kashmiris, and some Indians and Pakistanis alike. While it may be too early to answer the question, it is important to ask whether this devastating earthquake will have permanent import for the strained détente.

Beginning with pre-independence and concluding with the most recent normalization efforts, Ambassador Dennis Kux provides an extensive analysis and comparison of key negotiations between India and Pakistan. Although numerous volumes analyze contentious bilateral issues, such as Kashmir and the two countries' respective nuclear weapons programs, little scholarship explains how the countries have negotiated through these issues.

This volume contains the historical foundation and detailed analysis of successful, stagnant, and failed India-Pakistan negotiations. Ambassador Kux presents the India-Pakistan relationship in terms of three topics: "problem-solving negotiations" with the 1960 Indus Waters Treaty and the 1962–1963 talks on Kashmir; "postconflict negotiations" regarding the 1966 Tashkent and 1972 Simla summits; and "talks about talks," or the 1999 Lahore and 2001 Agra summits working toward normalization. Ambassador Kux compares the political intuitions, diplomatic, tactics and leadership styles between and within the two countries. He also explains the evolving role of the media, external players (British, American, and Soviet), and cultural differences in the bilateral negotiations.

Ambassador Kux's volume comes out of the United States Institute of Peace Center for Conflict Analysis and Prevention (formerly Research and

Studies). The impetus for this work is based on the Institute's commitment both to understanding the cross-cultural dynamics of negotiating relationships and to making meaningful efforts to prevent future conflicts by negotiating differences. In advancement of both goals, the Institute has undertaken several initiatives to understand the nature of the security competition between India and Pakistan and to find novel ways of diminishing prospects for future conflict. Ambassador Kux's work is the most recent addition to a growing body of Institute-sponsored inquiries into South Asian regional stability, as well as studies of the negotiating dynamics between parties in conflict. (See Tamara Cofman Wittes' study *How Israelis and Palestinians Negotiate: A Cross-Cultural Analysis of the Oslo Peace Process*, Washington, DC: USIP Press, March 2005.)

As part of the Institute's continued examination of peaceful approaches to conflict resolution through dialogue and training, the study concludes with lessons learned from these six negotiation experiences as well as the prospects and vulnerabilities of the current negotiating process. The current thaw may represent the final step to cement nascent bilateral cooperation between New Delhi and Islamabad on such issues as trade, natural resource management, counterterrorism, cross-border movements, and cultural understanding. However, Ambassador Dennis Kux reminds us that their complex bilateral history makes it premature to conclude that India and Pakistan can create a lasting peace and normal interstate relations.

Richard H. Solomon, President
United States Institute of Peace

SUMMARY

India and Pakistan gained their independence in August 1947 ending two centuries of British imperial rule. Despite occasional periods of détente, such as the present thaw, their relations as independent nation-states have been frosty and tense. Their hostilities have led them to three wars, the Kargil crisis, and several near conflicts. They have sought periodically—without notable success—to achieve friendlier relations through negotiations.

Procedurally, the current normalization effort, which began two years ago, follows a concept called the "composite dialogue" agreed upon in the mid-1990s. This calls for separate, but parallel, talks on different bilateral issues, including the Kashmir dispute. Substantively, the current negotiations have made progress, and India-Pakistan relations are better than they have been in many years. However, the road to full normalization, including a Kashmir settlement, is long and full of barriers. If this study's review of past India-Pakistan negotiations has any lessons—and history usually does—vigorous, innovative, and sustained leadership will be required of both India and Pakistan to achieve tangible, across-the-board improvement in bilateral relations. Otherwise, at some point the present endeavor will run into the sand like previous efforts.

Given the importance of India and Pakistan as accounting for nearly 20 percent of humanity as well as being nuclear weapon states and having a strained relationship that threatens Asian and global stability, surprisingly little has been written about their negotiating experience. Library shelves sag with the heft of volumes about the Kashmir dispute. There are also weighty tomes about the two countries' nuclear weapons programs. Numerous accounts regard India-Pakistan conflicts and near conflicts, but no serious analysis exists on how the two nuclear-armed protagonists have negotiated with each other. Under the auspices of the United States Institute of Peace (USIP), this study tries to fill the void by providing an overview of six key India-Pakistan negotiations. This analysis will hopefully encourage others to probe the subject in greater depth because the India-Pakistan negotiating experience warrants far more attention than it has received.

HISTORICAL REVIEW

The study begins with consideration of the critical decades before the British left the subcontinent in 1947 and the events of that traumatic year. To understand postindependence India-Pakistan interaction, a solid comprehension of what occurred during British colonial rule is critical, especially the ten decisive years that preceded partition of British India into two independent states. The dramatic and sad events linked to the actual separation in 1947 also require close scrutiny. These events cast a long and dark shadow over India-Pakistan dealings. Indeed, a strong argument can be made that post-independence diplomatic failures have largely been a continuation in another form of the impasse between the Muslim League and Indian National Congress in their on-again, off-again negotiations between 1937 and 1947.

ANALYSIS OF SIX CRITICAL INDIA-PAKISTAN NEGOTIATIONS

The study then reviews six of the most important negotiations since independence. These provide valuable lessons and a better understanding of how India and Pakistan have dealt with each other across the bargaining table. Several of the negotiations achieved short-term successes but then failed to effect lasting improvement in relations. The Indus Waters negotiations is the only one that has achieved, and so far endured, its principal objective—to solve the dispute over how India and Pakistan would share the waters of the Indus River and its tributaries. The six negotiations are considered chronologically but are also grouped into the following three categories for analytical purposes:

❖ problem-solving negotiations (1960 Indus Waters Treaty and the 1962–1963 talks aimed at solving the Kashmir problem),

❖ postconflict negotiations (1966 Tashkent and 1972 Simla summits), and

❖ "Talks about Talks" (1999 Lahore and 2001 Agra summits).

The study concludes with a discussion of lessons learned from these six negotiation patterns and styles, such as the impact of cultural differences, as well as prospects that the current negotiating process will not repeat the two countries' previous lack of success.[i]

India-Pakistan Negotiations

Is Past Still Prologue?

1

From the Raj to India and Pakistan

The Slow March toward Self-rule

As the twentieth century began, the British Raj stood at its zenith. A few thousand British administrators in the Imperial Civil Service ruled India in a manner that was in keeping with the imperialist spirit of that era but out of tune with Britain's parliamentary democracy. At the high noon of empire, the Viceroy sat atop the Imperial Administration in Calcutta with his counterpart in London, the Secretary of State, who were jointly responsible for India's governance and welfare to the British parliament. They were not responsible, however, to the people of India.

Four decades after the Mutiny of 1857–58, which Indian and Pakistani nationalists call the First War of Independence, the British had full control over India, and the country seemed stable and calm, though poor. The British directly administered two-thirds of the territory, and more than 500 Indian princes ruled the remaining one-third as British residents kept a watchful eye. The larger principalities, for example Jammu and Kashmir in the North and Hyderabad in the South, would have been substantial nation-states if independent.

In 1885, the first green shoots of Indian nationalism began to sprout with the formation of the Indian National Congress (the Congress). Drawing inspiration from British liberalism, the Congress was initially an upper middle class organization and not anti-British. However, the Congress became increasingly critical of the Raj's ponderous pace of political reform and continued discrimination against Indians, especially their exclusion from the senior ranks of administration. Despite a considerable effort to attract Muslims, the Congress remained a largely Hindu organization. The Muslim upper classes had dominated most of the subcontinent for 600 years—from the victory of Mahmud of Ghori at Panipat in 1191 until the East India Company gained ascendancy after the battle of Plassey in 1757. Politically displaced by the British, the Muslim elite was psychologically bruised and slow to adjust to changed circumstances under the Raj. Hindus took far greater advantage of the new political, administrative, and educational opportunities that British India offered.

In 1901, India's 284 million people were predominantly Hindu. Muslims were about a quarter of the population. Smaller numbers of Christians, Sikhs, Buddhists, Parsis, tribals, and even a few Jews completed India's rich religious mix. Despite many differences and periodic communal disturbances, Hindus, Muslims, and the other minorities generally coexisted peacefully with each other. The small British ruling elite formed, in effect, a separate community that occupied the pinnacle of India's complex and highly stratified social and religious pyramid.

In 1907, a group of Muslim notables, led by the Agha Khan who was the wealthy leader of the Ismaili sect, founded the Muslim League (the League). Their purpose was to provide the community with a political voice, one that was both distinct from the Congress and less antagonistic toward the British. In response to Muslim entreaties, that same year the Viceroy Lord Minto announced that Muslims need not compete directly with the Hindu majority in elections as they would vote in separate electorates for Muslim candidates. Whether the product of imperial "divide and rule" strategy or of a genuine desire to ensure fairer representation for the Muslim minority, this action sharpened a sense of separate Hindu and Muslim political identities just as the electoral process was becoming more important. The Morely-Minto Indian Councils Act of 1909 substantially enlarged the role elections played in choosing Indian members of municipal, provincial, and even national level councils.[1]

One young anti-imperialist Muslim, Mohammed Ali Jinnah, already a prominent Bombay attorney and an elected member of the new Central Legislative Assembly, found the League too conservative and insufficiently nationalist. Jinnah became a Congress activist and worked hard to forge a program for Indian self-government that both Hindus and Muslims could support. In 1916, meeting at Lucknow, the Congress and the League adopted an accord that Jinnah helped to create. Through weighted voting and other political safeguards, the Lucknow Pact protected the rights of the Muslim minority in a post-British government of India.[2] A year later, at the height of World War I, Edwin Montagu, Secretary of State for India, declared it was British policy to move toward dominion status after the war. Given Montagu's pledge and the Hindu-Muslim political understanding

embodied in the Lucknow Pact, the road seemed clear for the early establishment of a self-governing Dominion of India.

This was not to be, however. Hindu-Muslim political unity proved too
fragile. Indian political leaders were unable to maintain a united front on
the question of safeguards for the Muslim minority. The Indian National
Congress withdrew support for separate electorates, but failed to reach
agreement on alternate arrangements that would have guaranteed 30 percent of legislative seats for Muslims which Jinnah and other Muslim leaders
sought. After Mohandas K. (Mahatma) Gandhi won the leadership of the
Congress, he transformed the organization into a mass nationalist movement that employed the strategy of passive resistance and noncooperation
to stir large-scale, but nonviolent agitation against the British. Although no
less nationalist than Gandhi, Jinnah's preference for legal and parliamentary pressures clashed with the Mahatma's populist vision of political
action. Theirs was never an easy relationship. As Gandhi's star rose, Jinnah
found himself increasingly sidelined in the Congress and finally left the
organization in 1921.[3]

An even more important obstacle to early self-rule was the hardening of
British policy. After World War I ended, London's enthusiasm for dominion status for India waned. The British only grudgingly expanded the scope
of self-government in the Montagu-Chelmsford reforms of 1919 and
extended drastic and unpopular wartime emergency powers through the
Rowlatt Acts. To undercut support for the Congress, the British emphasized
protection of political rights for the minorities and for the Indian princes.

Brushing aside Indian demands for early independence, London
marched to its own lumbering imperialist tempo. Between 1929 and 1931,
Indian political leaders and the highest levels of the British government
participated in three roundtable conferences. Gandhi created much sensa-
tion by attending meetings and having tea at Buckingham Palace with King
George V dressed in a traditional Indian *dhoti*, rather than a Western business suit. When the roundtable conferees failed to agree on a road map for
India's future, the British government implemented its own proposals.
The Parliament eventually approved the Government of India Act of
1935, which introduced full self-rule at the provincial level and envisaged
a federal structure for the central government. The British would continue
to exercise key functions at the center, but the elected national legislature

would have a greater role. Implementing the federal proposals required India's princes' approval. The 1935 Act, however, satisfied no one: not the Congress, the League, or hard-line British imperialists, such as Winston Churchill.

A year before, in 1934, a group of Indian Muslim students in England had made a radical proposal that called for the creation of a separate Muslim state called Pakistan (land of the pure) when the British finally left India. Initially, few took the Pakistan idea seriously, least of all Mohammed Ali Jinnah. By then, he was leading the League and trying to revive an organization that internal rivalries weakened. Despite chronic friction with Gandhi and other Congress chiefs over minority safeguards and their strikingly different political styles, Jinnah continued to regard Hindu-Muslim cooperation and a united India as the essential cornerstone for a stable post-British political future. Few would have imagined that within a decade the Muslim League leader would become the driving wedge splitting India into two states.

1937—1947: United India after the Raj?

The 1935 Act entered into effect and India went to the polls in 1937 to elect provincial legislatures. The Congress joined the electoral process only after considerable hesitation, yet swept the balloting for the so-called general seats and won majorities in eight of eleven provinces. The League fared poorly in the separate voting for Muslim seats in the provinces where Muslims formed a majority of the population including the Punjab, Bengal, Sind, and the Northwest Frontier Province. The League did more creditably where Muslims were a significant minority, in the United Provinces (UP, now Uttar Pradesh) and the Bombay Presidency (now Gujarat and Maharastra).

At this point, the Congress fatefully spurned coalition feelers from the League in UP and Bombay. Congress offered two ministerial posts in UP, but only if the provincial League would agree to merge. When the League refused to give up its separate organizational identity, Muslims found themselves shut out of political power in India's largest province. The Congress leadership also frustrated feelers about a possible coalition in Bombay. Events in UP and Bombay stoked fear among Muslims about their fate if the Congress were to succeed the British as rulers of India.[4] Concerns were aggravated when the Congress ministries suggested that there would be a considerable Hindu flavor in an independent India. The Congress decision to launch a mass campaign to attract Muslim members also angered Jinnah. This action undercut his own efforts to build up the League as the political voice of the Muslims of India.

In response, Jinnah and his colleagues decided upon a radical change in strategy that set India on the road to partition. The League no longer sought cooperation between Hindus and Muslims. Instead, it adopted the opposite approach by stressing intercommunal differences. The former leading spokesman for Hindu-Muslim unity became the articulate preacher of disunity. After 1938, Jinnah and other League leaders hammered away at the importance of not replacing British imperialism with "Hindu imperialism," or to put it another way, the British Raj with the Hindu Raj. To mobilize political support among the poor Muslim masses, the League stirred religious sentiments by adopting the emotionally charged slogan of "Islam in danger" in a Hindu-dominated India.

To buttress his case, Jinnah argued the view that India was not one, but two, nations: a Hindu India and a Muslim India:

The Hindus and Muslims belong to two different religious philosophies, social customs, and literature. They neither intermarry, nor interdine *[sic]* together and indeed they belong to two different civilizations which are mainly based on conflicting ideas and conception . . . Their aspects on life and of life are different . . . They have different epics, their heroes are different, and likewise their victories and defeats overlap. To yoke together two such nations under a single state, one as a numerical minority and the other as a majority, must lead to growing discontent and final destruction of any fabric that may be built up for the government of that state.[5]

The Congress flatly rejected the two-nation theory.[6] Mahatma Gandhi fiercely opposed splitting India on religious lines. He argued that once India was free of the British, it would provide a democratic and tolerant home for all minorities, including Muslims. His apparent political heir, Jawaharlal Nehru, regarded Jinnah's stance as reactionary and opportunistic.

Whatever the merits of the anti-Hindu, Muslim-mobilization campaign, the League's membership rapidly grew in response to the cry of "Islam in danger." While the League was transforming itself into a mass organization, its leaders were debating what sort of political arrangement they should seek in a post-British India. Ultimately, the League came around to supporting the idea of a separate homeland for Muslims. On March 23, 1940, the League formally adopted the Pakistan resolution at its annual gathering in Lahore. At the time many thought the campaign for Pakistan was more of a negotiating tactic to achieve broader minority rights and safeguards than a genuine political goal.

By then, the provisions of the Government of India Act of 1935 relating to the central government had been shelved. As the Indian princes failed to give the required assent for the proposed federal structure, this part of the 1935 Act was not implemented, even though the provisions for full provincial autonomy had already been put into effect. In September 1939, the British Viceroy Lord Linlithgow simply announced that the federal provisions of the 1935 Act had lapsed. As a result, the British retained full executive control at the center during World War II. When the conflict ended in 1945, the Congress and the League, as India's two leading and increasingly polarized, nationalist movements, faced the daunting challenge of agreeing to a political structure for India's post-British government. Had the 1935 Act been fully implemented in the late 1930s, India would have had a functioning federal system and what amounted to a constitution already in place. History might have taken a different course.

The prospects of the Pakistan movement received a major boost during the war when the Congress refused support for the Allied effort unless the British took significant steps to increase Indian participation in the central government. Despite pressure from U.S. President Franklin D. Roosevelt, Prime Minister Winston Churchill offered little more than token concessions. In response, the Congress decided to launch a noncooperation campaign in August 1942 to impel the British to "Quit India." The British authorities responded by arresting the senior Congress leadership and thousands of party activists. Coinciding with the low point in the Allied struggle against Germany and Japan, the "Quit India" movement cost the Congress what little sympathy it had with the British. While the Congress chiefs languished in jail, Jinnah and other League leaders supporting the war effort were free to propagate the Pakistan cause throughout India. As Punjabi Muslims constituted the largest element of the British Indian Army, the British treated Jinnah with considerable care and were careful not to upset Muslim feelings.

In September 1944, Jinnah and Gandhi, who had been released from custody for health reasons, discussed a political formula that would permit contiguous Muslim majority districts in northwest and northeast India to become separate states if their populations voted for independence. The talks broke down when Jinnah insisted that the provinces of Bengal and the Punjab, where Muslims were a small majority, vote as a unit. Jinnah complained that voting by district would result in "a shadow of a husk" or "a moth-eaten Pakistan." In fact, this is exactly what happened in 1947 when the Punjab and Bengal were split between India and Pakistan. Gandhi's willingness to negotiate with Jinnah boosted the League leader's political standing and his claim to speak for India's Muslims.

With victory over the Axis powers in sight in early 1945, the British released the other Congress leaders from custody. Linlithgow's successor as Viceroy, Lord Archibald Wavell, previously commander-in-chief of the Indian Army, tried unsuccessfully to establish an interim national government. In the negotiations at Simla that followed, the Congress was willing to accept equal cabinet representation for Hindus and Muslims even though the latter represented only a quarter of India's population. When Jinnah insisted that the League nominate all the Muslim cabinet members, the talks collapsed.

That summer, Word War II ended with Japan's surrender. In Britain, the Labour Party swept Winston Churchill and the Conservatives from power in parliamentary elections. Unlike the Conservatives, Labour favored early independence for India. It was no longer a question of if or when the British would leave, but rather how, especially regarding the future political structures and arrangements. New elections were held in the winter of 1945–46 to provide a fresh mandate for the provincial governments and to select a constituent assembly to write a constitution for an independent India. The results enormously strengthened the League's hand and the credibility of the demand for Pakistan. In contrast to its modest showing in 1937, the League won all the Muslim seats in the constituent assembly along with 446 of the 495 Muslim provincial assembly seats. This greatly reinforced Jinnah's claim that he spoke politically for the Muslims of India.

In the spring of 1946, the Labour government sent a Cabinet Mission to India in an effort to find a political formula that would maintain India's unity. When the Congress and League failed to agree, the Cabinet Mission tabled its own plan. This called for a federal structure with a weak central government and three politically strong regional entities. Two of these, located in the northwest and northeast, would have Muslim majorities. On June 6, 1946, the League surprised observers by agreeing to the Cabinet Mission plan. Until then, Jinnah had tenaciously insisted that nothing less than full separation would be acceptable. When the Congress appeared to follow suit, it looked as if the future of India was settled, and the country would remain united after the British left.

Smiles quickly faded. Nehru, in particular, damaged matters by making public statements to the effect that the Congress was not irrevocably committed to the Cabinet Mission plan. "What we do there [in the Constituent Assembly], we are entirely and absolutely free to determine. We have committed ourselves on no single matter to anybody," the Congress leader stated.[7] In fact, Nehru and the Congress wanted a stronger central government than the one the Cabinet Mission envisaged, and they disliked the provisions in the plan that permitted a regional grouping to secede after a ten-year period. It is impossible to know if the structure the Cabinet Mission proposed would have proven workable, but the unwillingness of the Congress to commit itself unequivocally rang the death knell on a united India.

Jinnah, who had come under fire for having accepted less than a fully independent Pakistan, reacted furiously. At his urging, the League withdrew its endorsement of the Cabinet Mission plan. Until then, he had been a stickler for legal niceties. Now Jinnah called for "direct action to achieve Pakistan," telling the League Working Committee on July 29, 1946:

> Today, we have said good-bye to constitutional methods and talks . . . I am also going to make trouble now. Throughout the painful negotiations, the two parties (the Congress and the British) with whom we bargained held a pistol at us; one with power and machines at us; and the other with non-cooperation and the threat to launch a mass civil disobedience. This situation must be met. We also have a pistol.[8]

This decisive change in League tactics sparked violent pro-Pakistan demonstrations on August 16, 1946, in Calcutta that left an estimated 5,000 dead and 15,000 injured. The Calcutta riots raised the curtain on tragic communal mayhem that spread like plague through many parts of India in the final sad year of the British Raj. Although an interim government was eventually established with Nehru as prime minister and Jinnah's deputy Liaquat Ali Khan as finance minister, there was scant cooperation and constant friction between Congress and League ministers. In December 1946, with the political impasse hardening, a desperate British Prime Minister Clement Attlee summoned to London Jinnah and Liaquat, Congress chiefs Nehru and Sardar Patel, and the Sikh leader Baldev Singh. Gandhi had by then semi-retired from active politics. The discussions proved fruitless as the gap between the League and the Congress had become too wide to bridge.

Worried about their ability to maintain law and order, the British decided on shock therapy. In February 1947, Attlee announced that the Raj would end in June 1948 whether or not there was agreement on political arrangements. Lord Louis Mountbatten, a cousin of King George VI, replaced Wavell as Viceroy. On reaching India, Mountbatten quickly decided that partition was inevitable and that the date for independence should be advanced by nearly a full year to August 1947. The British hoped this action would defuse communal unrest and focus the attention of Indian leaders on the issues of post-Raj governance, rather than on arguing with each other.

On June 3, 1947, both the Congress and the League reluctantly accepted Mountbatten's proposal, which included partition of Bengal and the Punjab if the provincial assemblies so voted. By then, the Congress leadership had concluded that dividing India into two countries was perhaps the only way to prevent civil war and to ensure the early departure of the British. Jinnah and the League judged that a "moth-eaten Pakistan" was the best that could be achieved under the circumstances.

The Year 1947: The Transfer of Power and Partition

Advancing the British departure by a year meant that there was less than three months, in fact only seventy-two days, to complete the awesome task of dividing the Indian Empire into two separate and independent states. This involved splitting the major functions of the country into two parts, including partitioning the Punjab and Bengal provinces, dividing financial and other national assets, establishing two separate administrative structures, dividing the Indian Army, Navy, and Air Force, deciding how to manage the vast Indus River irrigation system that straddled the likely frontiers, fixing the boundaries of India and Pakistan, and resolving the fate of the princely states that comprised a third of British India. In theory, though not in practice, the princely states would regain independence when the Raj ended.

British haste to leave made it impossible to complete the transitional process in any kind of orderly manner. The precipitous departure caused problems that enormously complicated subsequent India-Pakistan bilateral relations, including triggering the traumatic and tragic flight of 15 million refugees, stirring animosity between former civil service colleagues, and causing the dispute over the fate of the princely state of Jammu and Kashmir that still remains unresolved a half century later. Mountbatten's unwise action simply did not allow sufficient time to settle the myriad of complex and difficult issues that establishing two separate nation-states entailed.

Partition of the Punjab

The problems at the national level were paralleled at the provincial level in the Punjab and in Bengal, where the provinces themselves were partitioned. Emotions ran especially high in the Punjab among Hindus, Muslims, and several million vehemently anti-Pakistan Sikhs. Many worried about serious trouble as independence approached. Reality proved far worse than the most pessimistic fears. Near open warfare broke out, triggering an unplanned and chaotic mass exodus of perhaps seven million fearful Hindus and Sikhs from the western Punjab that became part of Pakistan, and of a similar number of terrified Muslims from the eastern Punjab that remained with India. The final location of the border between India and Pakistan in the Punjab was not announced until after independence, ratcheting already soaring uncertainties. Although Bengal was also partitioned and suffered from communal disturbances, these were of much lesser intensity than the Punjab calamity. A large Hindu minority—perhaps 10 percent of the population—remained in what became Pakistan's east wing or East Bengal. Only a handful of Hindus or Sikhs remained in Pakistani Punjab.

By 1960, virtually all the vexing administrative problems associated with the splitting of British India into two countries had been settled. As one of the most difficult challenges, the Indus Waters Treaty sucessfully dealt with the Indus River canal irrigation system in September 1960, but this was after eight years of difficult negotiations and with the help of the World Bank. However, the trauma of partition left lasting emotional scars on both sides of the border. Perhaps 500,000 people died as millions fled their homes to escape what amounted to ethnic cleansing. They were forced to create new lives for themselves and their families under the most trying circumstances. Even two generations after the integration of refugees into their new homelands, the horror of 1947 is seared into the historical memory of millions of Indians and Pakistanis and has remained to be a tremendous psychological strain on the bilateral relationship.

Acrimony among Former Civil Service Colleagues

In the final seventy-two days of the Raj, Indian civil servants, both Muslim and Hindu, worked feverishly to resolve a myriad of technical and administrative issues. In addressing all politically sensitive tasks, such as deciding on the boundary between the two states, the civil servants proved no more able to reach agreement than the Congress and the League leadership. Former colleagues became bitter antagonists on opposite sides of the bargaining table, pressing hard to advance the interests of their new Indian and Pakistani masters. As the date for independence neared, tensions mounted.

In the case of the Boundary Commission, the Hindu and Muslim members disagreed on every sensitive issue. The Chairman, Sir Cyril Radcliffe, a prominent English lawyer with no previous India experience whose appointment Jinnah had suggested, had to cast the deciding vote on the frontier boundaries. Other key subjects, such as the division of financial assets and military equipment and supplies, were only settled after partition and often with great acrimony. The Pakistanis firmly believed that the Indians had shortchanged them in the transfer of military assets. Mahatma Gandhi had to threaten to start one of his famous fasts before the new Congress-led Government of India would agree to transfer Pakistan's share of the national treasury.

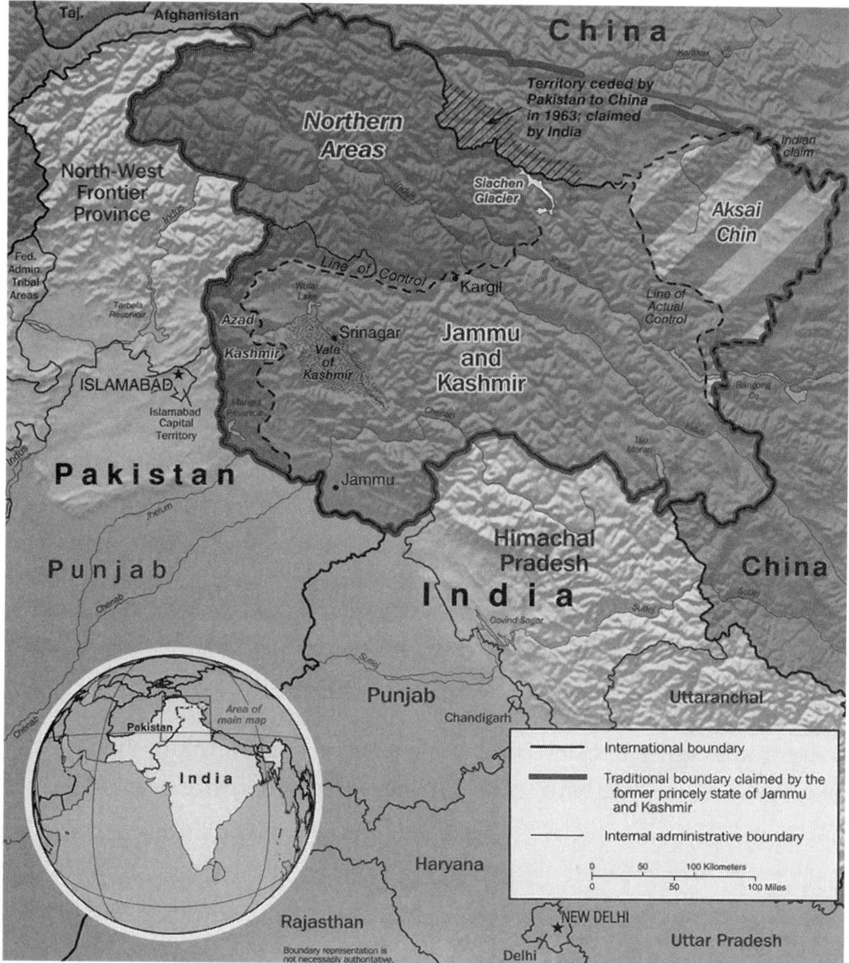

The Kashmir Dispute

One of the worst and longest-lasting problems that the British bequeathed to India and Pakistan was the dispute over Kashmir. In the final days of the Raj, Mountbatten strongly encouraged, but did not compel, the princes to join either India or Pakistan. The rulers based their decision on two principal criteria: geography and the communal composition of their populations. Although in theory independence was feasible for the largest states, the British stressed this was not an option. Again, insufficient time meant that the British departed India without settling this issue, forcing the fledgling governments of India and Pakistan to address the politically explosive problem.

Before August 14–15, 1947, almost all rulers signed instruments of accession in keeping with the recommended criteria. Unfortunately, the two largest princely states failed to act: Hyderabad with a Muslim ruler and a mainly Hindu population, and Jammu and Kashmir with a Hindu ruler and Muslim majority. They fell into a legal vacuum after the departure of the British. Located in south central India, Hyderabad was entirely surrounded by India. In September 1948, New Delhi forcibly incorporated the state.

Strategically located in the Himalayas in the North, Jammu and Kashmir proved harder to resolve. Although the state bordered Pakistan and India (the latter only because the Radcliffe Commission Boundary Award provided a slender physical link with India), Kashmir's all-weather road connections and its commercial ties were with Pakistan. According to the recommended criteria, Kashmir should have become part of Pakistan as a contiguous Muslim-majority state. However, an array of circumstances kept the issue from being settled so easily. The Maharajah was a Hindu and not eager to join Pakistan. Kashmir's most popular political leader, Sheikh Mohammed Abdullah, and his party, the National Conference, had close ties with the Indian National Congress and did not want to join Pakistan. Finally, India's Prime Minister Jawaharlal Nehru, whose family belonged to the Kashmiri Brahmin subcaste, had an emotional attachment to the homeland of his ancestors.

Two months after independence, at the end of October 1947, Kashmir's unresolved status triggered a mini-war and the dispute that has soured India-Pakistan relations for more half a century. When the Maharajah equivocated about joining either country, the Pakistanis took matters into their own hands by sending tribal irregulars from the Northwest Frontier Province to attempt to seize the state by force. At this point, the panicked Maharajah signed the document of accession to India.

Legally speaking, the Maharajah's action settled matters and made Jammu and Kashmir a part of the Indian Union. Ever a stickler for legalism, Jinnah had maintained that the accession decision lay entirely in the hands of the rulers of princely states and was not dependent on popular will.

Thus, he had accepted the accession to Pakistan of the Muslim ruler of the small state of Junagadh, located on the western coast of India, despite its lack of contiguous borders with Pakistan and its predominantly Hindu population. India promptly occupied the state and a "plebiscite" ratified a decision to join the Indian Union.

In Kashmir, a hurriedly assembled Indian military force was able to stem the raiders' advance and push them out of the Srinagar Valley—the heart of the state where most speakers of the Kashmiri language live. India brought the Kashmir problem to the United Nations Security Council in January 1948. After a year of deliberations, the Council was able to achieve a cease-fire that entered into force on January 1, 1949. India controlled the southern two-thirds of Kashmir, including the Srinagar Valley. Pakistan ended up with the northern third of the state. More than half a century later, the division remains largely unaltered.

THE BURDEN OF HISTORY

When the Union Jack was lowered in Karachi in the morning of August 14, 1947 and in New Delhi at the stroke of midnight, Pakistan and India began their existence as independent nation-states burdened by a legacy of mutual distrust and antagonism. The political rights of the Muslim minority occupied a central place in the deliberations about India's political future during the half-century before independence. Initially, Indian nationalists and Hindu and Muslim leaders worked together in negotiating with the British to end the Raj and to achieve self-government. However, the intercommunal unity reflected in the 1916 Lucknow Pact broke down during the 1920s. In the decisive stage of negotiations between 1937 and 1947, one had a peculiar situation of the Congress and the League both wanting the British to leave, but vehemently opposed to each other. They ultimately offered two different and conflicting visions of a post-British India.

This led to an unusually complex series of negotiations, especially in the post-1945 period when the British were no longer dragging their feet to retain power in India. In these three-cornered talks, London at first sought a formula that would be acceptable to both the Congress and the League, yet maintain India's unity. In the end, fearful of a collapse of British authority, London accepted the partition of its Indian Empire. Interestingly, the key participants in the negotiations on the Indian side were all lawyers and supporters of the parliamentary system, Gandhi, Nehru, and Patel in the Congress and Jinnah and Liaquat Ali Khan in the Muslim League. Nonetheless, first the Congress and then, after 1937, the League were prepared to adopt extra-parliamentary tactics to rouse mass support for their respective causes. The Congress suspected, particularly Nehru, that the British were manipulating the postwar negotiations in order to maintain some sort of strategic foothold in South Asia after independence, which was another complicating factor.

The angry Congress-League disputes in the decade leading up to independence and the traumatic events of 1947 set the stage for India and Pakistan's inability to live with one another in a reasonably amicable fashion. Their inability to agree on postindependence arrangements foreshadowed their failure to resolve bilateral problems through diplomacy and negotiation. After a decade of bitter arguments, it was difficult, perhaps impossible, for Jinnah, Nehru, Liaquat, Patel, and other political leaders to suddenly shift gears and to embrace those whom they had come to regard with deep mistrust and contempt.

The League's strategy of stirring fear of Hindu domination was successful in quickly mobilizing mass support for a separate Muslim state. Jinnah's tenacity helped achieve what few thought was possible in the late 1930s. In his much-quoted speech to the Pakistan Constituent Assembly on August 11, 1947, Jinnah urged his countrymen and women to put the past behind them and to regard all citizens, whether Muslim, Hindu, Christian, or other minorities as loyal Pakistanis. However, ten years of strident, high-pitched anti-Hindu and anti-Congress agitation could not be turned off like a water tap. After the events of 1947, this attitude hardened into an entrenched aversion of the Pakistani leadership toward India. There was genuine fear that the far larger neighbor was not only hostile, but also intent on doing in Pakistan through undoing the partition by turning the new country into a de facto appendage. In this vein as late as December 1965, President Ayub Khan told President Lyndon Johnson, "I know you won't believe it but those Indians are going to gobble us up."[9] Pakistan had become, as Thomas Thornton aptly put it, an "insecurity state."[10]

In the case of India, the sharply negative attitude of the Congress leaders toward the League evolved into a similarly negative attitude toward Pakistan. Before independence, there was disdain and disbelief regarding the two-nation theory and, until the 1945–46 elections, scorn for the League's claim to represent the Muslims of India. Jinnah's call to split India along religious lines was anathema to the Congress chiefs. An agnostic with little taste for any religion and visceral opposition to appeals to communal feelings, Nehru thoroughly disliked Jinnah. The League leader reciprocated these sentiments.

Although Nehru accepted Pakistan as an unpleasant fact, he never really believed that it was desirable. Also, he doubted in the first years of independence whether the new country would endure. Nehru's talks with senior U.S. leaders, including Presidents Truman and Eisenhower as well as Secretaries of State George Marshall, Dean Acheson, and John Foster Dulles, clearly expressed the Indian leader's antipathy toward the concept of Pakistan. He also conveyed belief that its leadership was obscurantist and venomously prejudiced against India.[11]

Events since independence have perpetuated and even intensified hostility, thus further impairing prospects for amicable India-Pakistan diplomatic dealings. First, the India-Pakistan war occurred in 1965. Then, the 1971 conflict broke off East Pakistan into Bangladesh as an independent country. During the 1980s, Pakistan provided covert support, such as arms, intelligence, and training to Sikh separatists. Since 1990, Pakistan has supported the anti-India Kashmir insurgency and the 1999 Kargil mini-war. Most recently, the 2002–03 military mobilization after Islamic terrorists sought to storm the Indian Parliament caused a near war. Despite occasional periods of détente, a series of postindependence conflicts show that India and Pakistan have remained locked in a South Asian cold war for more than fifty years. The current thaw and bilateral "composite dialogue" may conceivably represent a turning point, but it is too soon to conclude that India and Pakistan will succeed in establishing a more peaceful and normal relationship.

2

THE INDIA-PAKISTAN NEGOTIATING EXPERIENCE

Since 1947, India and Pakistan have negotiated over scores of issues countless times. These have ranged from minor technical questions, such as border railway crossings and timetables, to highly contentious political questions of vital national security interests, such as nuclear confidence-building measures and the Kashmir dispute. This study reviews six of the most important and best-known India-Pakistan negotiations. Others could have been added, for example, refugee property negotiations in the late 1940s and 1950s, the unsuccessful 1954 India-Pakistan talks on Kashmir, the Benazir Bhutto-Rajiv Gandhi parlays of the late 1980s, and the discussions between Pakistan's Nawaz Sharif and India's Inder K. Gujral in the mid-1990s. However, including these and other negotiations would have transformed what is intended as an introductory examination into a full-fledged survey that would have run several hundred pages.

These six cases can provide a preliminary assessment of the India-Pakistan negotiating process and experience. Although there are different prisms through which to analyze the negotiations, these six cases are effective examples according to their purpose: solving a specific problem, trying to normalize relations in a postconflict situation, and establishing a joint framework for future negotiations that address India-Pakistan differences.[12]

The successful Canal Waters negotiations ended in agreement on the Indus Waters Treaty. In contrast, the Kashmir talks failed. Both negotiations involved intense external involvement—the World Bank in dealing with the Indus waters and high-level U.S. and U.K. engagement during the Kashmir talks. The Indus Waters negotiations began in 1952 and lasted for eight years before the treaty was signed in September 1960. The Kashmir negotiations began in December 1962 and ended after six months and six rounds in May 1963.

The second category of negotiations involves efforts to reestablish normal relations after India-Pakistan wars. The Tashkent conference followed the 1965 conflict and the summit at Simla after the 1971 War.[13] The two summits achieved their limited objective of restoring the status quo ante bellum, but neither was able to achieve the larger goal of establishing a sustained process of India-Pakistan normalization negotiations. Although the two governments agreed on this aim, they failed to follow through. At Tashkent, the Soviets were a central participant, hosting the conference and providing active and highest level good offices. Simla was a strictly bilateral India-Pakistan affair.

The third category of negotiations, the Lahore and Agra summits, can be described as "talks about talks." These negotiations involved Indian and Pakistani leaders attempting to reach agreement on a structured dialogue for future talks in the hope that this would achieve less tense bilateral tensions, lead to genuine détente, and eventually resolve all problems, including Kashmir. At the Lahore summit in February 1999, the two countries agreed on the process, but Pakistan's incursion across the Kashmir Line of Control (LOC) near Kargil derailed the dialogue. Two years later, in July 2001, the Agra summit proved an embarrassing failure as it ended acrimoniously with neither a joint statement nor agreement on a process for bilateral talks.

The political structures of India and Pakistan were carbon copies of each other in 1947, but over time they have diverged significantly. India has successfully institutionalized the parliamentary system and firmly established its version of democratic governance. Power rests in the hands of a prime minister backed by a majority of the popularly elected House of Commons, *Lok Sabha* or the House of the People. The Cabinet Committee on Security makes key foreign policy and national security decisions. Senior civil servants and representatives of defense services and intelligence agencies take part in the deliberations, but are clearly subordinate to the political leadership. The Indian military has remained under firm civilian control. Civilian scientists developed India's nuclear weapons. The military became part of the process only after the 1998 weapons tests.

Pakistan has followed a very different road. Since General Ayub Khan seized power in October 1958, the generals have controlled foreign and national security policy or had a veto, except for 1972–77 when civilian Zulfikar Ali Bhutto was in charge—first as president and chief martial law administrator and then after 1973 as prime minister. Since the military takeover of October 1999, President and Army Chief General Pervez Musharraf has been Pakistan's dominant political actor. Decision making in foreign affairs and national security matters rests in his hands and those of senior army colleagues. The civilian prime minister and the elected National Assembly have little involvement. Civilian scientists developed Pakistan's nuclear weapons, but under the army's direction and presumed control.

India and Pakistan's foreign ministries[14] operate in roughly parallel fashion, and the two countries follow similar procedures in managing their diplomacy. Both have adopted the organizational model of the British Foreign Office. The foreign ministers, at times supported by ministers of state, are political appointees with varying degrees of influence. In India, Nehru served as his own foreign minister from independence until his death in 1964. His daughter Indira Gandhi dominated policy making and her foreign ministers had little independence and limited influence. In recent years, some foreign ministers, for example, Inder K. Gujral and Jaswant Singh have been senior policy voices in India. In Pakistan, Z.A. Bhutto, as foreign minister under Ayub, had considerable influence. Similarly, Sahibzada Yaqub Khan, a retired Lt. General, serving during the 1980s under Zia-ul Haq, was a significant voice on the policymaking team.

Professional diplomats enter the Foreign Service through stiff competitive examinations in both foreign ministries. The number of career officers is relatively small, and they are highly qualified. Management and direction of each ministry rests in the hands of the foreign secretary, usually the most senior career diplomat. In India, because the retirement age is rigidly implemented (now sixty, but fifty-eight until a few years ago), there is often a rapid turnover in senior positions. In Pakistan, foreign secretaries usually enjoy longer tours and have often been kept on beyond retirement age. The ministries are organized along geographic and functional lines with subgroups led by secretaries or additional secretaries, all senior career officers. In India, the key player and policy coordinator for policy toward Pakistan is the joint secretary for Pakistan—organizationally equivalent to an assistant secretary in the U.S. State Department. In Pakistan, the equivalent position for its policy toward India is called the director-general for

South Asia. Both of these officials are involved in almost all governmental activities and negotiations with their neighbor.

Both ministries have earned reputations as strongholds of the status quo and opponents of policy innovation and change. The past fifty years of nearly unbroken bilateral hostility partly explains this inertia, but the conservative nature of Indian and Pakistani bureaucracies also contribute to the gridlock. Both India and Pakistan have conducted their bilateral negotiations with a great deal of stability and predictability. Each side has copious files regarding past dealings and is acutely aware of the negotiating record, or at least its respective version. Decisions on all India-Pakistan questions do not rest, however, with foreign ministry career officials. They are taken at the top levels of government. In both New Delhi and Islamabad, even relatively minor bilateral issues are considered matters of highest priority. The pattern is quite similar to the manner in which the United States and the Soviet Union managed issues during the Cold War. The major difference between the two countries is that in Pakistan, the military plays a key role in these decisions; whereas, in India the political leadership decides.

PROBLEM-SOLVING NEGOTIATIONS

The Indus Waters Treaty, September 1960

President Dwight D. Eisenhower began his September 9, 1960, press conference by stating, "In a very depressing world picture that we so often see there is one bright spot that seems to me worthy of mention and that is the settling of the Indus River Water problem between India and Pakistan."[15] Ten days later, Prime Minister Nehru and President Ayub Khan signed the Indus Waters Treaty in Karachi, then the capital of Pakistan. (Excerpts of the Indus Waters Treaty are found in appendix 1.) The agreement resolved a problem that if left unsettled, could have caused enormous economic damage for the western half of Pakistan. Unlike the Kashmir dispute that directly involved only a small minority of Indians and Pakistanis, the waters issue affected the lives of millions of people on both sides of the border.

The dispute concerned the management of one of the most significant achievements of the Raj—the vast irrigation system developed in the

Indus Valley. Tapping the waters of the Indus River and its five major tributaries—the Jhelum, Ravi, Chenab, Beas, and Sutlej rivers—the British developed a complex and extensive system of dams and canals to boost agricultural production by bringing river water to the semi-arid lands of the Punjab and Sind. The new frontier between India and Pakistan cut across the irrigation system. Many of the dams and canal headworks that stored or carried water to farmland in Pakistan were located in India. When the partition precipitously split British India into two countries in mid-1947, there was insufficient time to develop a new management structure. A prevailing, yet undue, optimism assumed that previous water-sharing arrangements could continue under an Inter-Dominion Accord signed in May 1948, despite the fact that a month before Indian Punjab had blocked the flow of water when its Pakistani counterpart did not pay its usage fees.

Maintaining the status quo would have required extraordinarily close cooperation between the two countries, something that was not realistically possible in the tense, post-August 1947 atmosphere. Moreover, Pakistan wanted to receive the same share of Indus Waters that it previously received. India sought a revised allocation system that would permit expanded irrigation on its side of the border. In particular, New Delhi wanted to build the long-discussed Bhakra Dam on the Sutlej River in order to produce more electric power and boost farm output. Pakistan vehemently objected to Bhakra, asserting that it would reduce the flow of water and gravely inhibit agriculture in the Pakistani Punjab and the princely state of Bahawalpur. India rejected Pakistan's call to allow the International Court of Justice to adjudicate their differences, and India urged a bilateral resolution of the problem.[16]

Matters remained at a standstill until August 1951 when David Lilienthal, former Chairman of the Tennessee Valley Authority and the U.S. Atomic Energy Commission, put forward a water-sharing proposal in *Colliers* magazine.[17] Lilienthal suggested that India and Pakistan jointly manage the waters system, and that this be substantially expanded with new dam and canal construction to increase the mutual benefits. The World Bank took up Lilienthal's idea, and India and Pakistan agreed to participate in technical discussions.

After the talks began in May 1952, with senior civil servants leading the delegations, it became apparent that the two countries continued to hold conflicting views over water allocation. Pakistan insisted that its prepartition share of the canal waters not be reduced. India urged a new concept. Two years later, in 1954, the World Bank assumed a more active role and tabled its own proposal in an effort to break the impasse. This envisaged splitting the system into two parts with India having exclusive use of the three eastern and Pakistan of the three western rivers. New canals and dams would divert water to Pakistan in order to replace flows lost in the process of division.

While Pakistan was unhappy with the proposal, which was closer to the Indian stance, it ultimately agreed to return to the bargaining table. Negotiations over the details dragged on for another six years until the parties reached final agreement in 1960.[18] Ultimately, India and Pakistan's willingness to address the issue as a technical problem, the World Bank's creative thinking, and the international community's generous financial support, especially from the United States, paved the way for a settlement.

The 1960 treaty divided the previously unified canal system into two separate entities. The waters of the three western rivers (the Indus, Jhelum, and Ravi) were entirely reserved for Pakistan and all the waters of the three eastern rivers (the Chenab, Beas, and Sutlej) were to be for India's exclusive use. In addition to maintaining existing flows for Pakistan, the treaty envisaged new dams and canals to permit a significant expansion of irrigation in both countries.[19] The cost of proposed construction came to U.S. $1.033 billion, a substantial sum in 1960. The United States underwrote U.S. $517 million, slightly more than half the total. The World Bank and other international donors shared the remainder.[20]

Why did the eight years of negotiation over the Indus Waters solve an extremely complex and economically explosive problem, while other negotiations, especially those dealing with Kashmir, have proven so unfruitful? The following are the key elements of success for the Indus Waters negotiations.

❖ Even though the economic and political stakes were extraordinarily high, the leadership of both countries agreed that the waters issue should be negotiated as a technical, not political, question.

❖ The political leadership in New Delhi and Karachi trusted their negotiators to see that vital national interests were protected in the bargain that ultimately emerged.

❖ Although Pakistan had to abandon its original position, it was ultimately willing to accept the essence of the World Bank's proposal. This did not reduce the flow of precious irrigation water and envisaged future growth.

❖ The World Bank was able to offer a large financial package to pay the costs of restructuring the existing irrigation system and also of developing substantial additional facilities. The tempting financial package encouraged the two sides, especially as India balked at compensating Pakistan. In the end, both sides could claim that they had gained, rather than lost through the negotiations.

❖ Members of the Indian and Pakistani teams had worked together in the administrative and irrigation services of British India. Both used familiar technical databases relating to the irrigation system. Thus, each side fully understood what the other was talking about, despite the technical complexities of the negotiations.

❖ The discussions stretched on for eight years, but remained out of the media limelight. This helped prevent the talks from becoming overly politicized despite the sensitivities of the issues being considered.

There was much wrangling during the lengthy negotiations. However, in the end, a bargain was struck that has held for more than four decades. Despite the India-Pakistan wars and crises since Nehru and Ayub signed the treaty in September 1960, the accord has continued. The two sides have sought to resolve Indus Waters differences in keeping with the relevant provisions of the treaty.

Currently, this dynamic is being tested with an issue relating to a power plant. Islamabad claims, and New Delhi denies, that construction of the Baglihar dam and hydroelectric plant in India's part of Kashmir is inconsistent with the treaty. After the two sides were unable to resolve the matter bilaterally, Pakistan invoked the dispute settlement provisions of the treaty. Pursuant to these, the World Bank chose a neutral expert to undertake a formal finding. The two countries are obligated to accept the forthcoming conclusion, and one side or the other may have to agree to modify its current stance, or otherwise jeopardize the stability and integrity of the 1960 treaty.

Negotiations on Kashmir, December 1962–May 1963

In the first fifteen years of independence, the United Nations, the United States, and the parties themselves all tried and failed to resolve the Kashmir dispute. Neither UN efforts in 1949, 1950, 1951–52, 1957, 1958, and 1961, American initiatives in 1949, 1953, and 1958, nor bilateral India-Pakistan talks in 1953 and 1954 could make any significant progress toward settling the dispute.

After John F. Kennedy became president in January 1961, he reluctantly agreed to wade into the Kashmir swamp. His initial effort went nowhere when India rejected his suggestion that former World Bank President Eugene Black serve as a mediator. Although Nehru respected Black, New Delhi had by then become allergic to third party involvement in the Kashmir issue. In mid-year 1962, Kennedy became engaged again as the United States supported a mildly worded UN Security Council resolution calling on India and Pakistan to hold direct negotiations on Kashmir. At India's behest, the Soviet Union vetoed the resolution.[21]

India's humiliating defeat in the October–November 1962 frontier war with China provided a fresh opportunity on Kashmir. When the United States and the United Kingdom proposed bilateral India-Pakistan negotiations, Ayub Khan readily agreed. Nehru could hardly refuse in view of India's sudden dependence on Western arms assistance. Lacking political will, however, the prime minister told the Indian Parliament that any change in the status of Kashmir would be "very bad for the people there." Only British Commonwealth Secretary Duncan Sandys' sudden visit to Delhi succeeded in having Nehru confirm his willingness to proceed with the negotiations without preconditions.[22] Veteran U.S. diplomat W. Averell Harriman, who had joined Sandys in South Asia, appraised the chances of successful Kashmir negotiations as "quite remote." Any accord to which either country would agree was unlikely to be acceptable to the other, Harriman warned Kennedy.[23]

Just before the negotiations were scheduled to begin, Pakistan upset matters by announcing an agreement to delineate the frontier of its part of Kashmir with China. Claiming Indian territory had been given away, New Delhi was furious (as was the United States).[24] Nonetheless, Nehru agreed to allow the talks to proceed. Prime Minister Swaran Singh, who previously served as India's railway minister, or foreign minister, led the Indian delegation, assisted by Foreign Secretary M. L. Gundevia. On the Pakistani side, Commerce and Industries Minister Zulfikar Ali Bhutto, a rising political star and a hardliner on India, stood in for ailing Foreign Minister Mohammed Ali Bogra and was seconded by Foreign Secretary S.K. Dehlavi. After Bogra died in January 1962, Bhutto became Pakistan's foreign minister.

The U.S. and U.K. envoys to Pakistan and India—respectively, Walter McConaughy and John Kenneth Galbraith, and Sir Morrice James and Paul Gore-Booth—closely shadowed the six rounds that shifted back and forth between major cities of the two countries. The diplomats conferred in detail with Indian and Pakistani officials before and after each round. President Kennedy and British Prime Minister Harold Macmillan sent a stream of messages to Ayub and Nehru in order to stress their personal interest, and to encourage the two sides to narrow the gap between their positions.

In the first round, held in Rawalpindi, Pakistan in late December 1962, the Indian and Pakistani teams reiterated their traditional positions on Kashmir. The second round in New Delhi, January 16–19, 1963, was more substantive. The negotiators discussed the possibility of an international boundary in Kashmir. As principles for the dividing line, the Pakistanis put forward composition of the population, security considerations, and control of the headwaters of the major rivers. The Indians objected to the first point lest it stir Hindu-Muslim communal troubles. Although they agreed that there should be an international boundary, the two sides ultimately failed to agree on how this should be accomplished.[25]

During the third round held in Karachi, India and Pakistan began drawing lines on the map. The Indians predictably proposed that the boundary should be the 1949 cease-fire line, with some modifications. Pakistan's counterproposal deeply disappointed Washington and angered New Delhi. Pakistan laid claim to almost all of the state, leaving India with only a sliver of Jammu.[26] Before the teams gathered for the fourth round in Calcutta, March 12–14, 1963, Pakistan soured matters further by announcing that Foreign Minister Bhutto would go to Beijing to sign the border agreement with China.

Even though Washington applied heavy pressure on Ayub to improve Pakistan's territorial proposal, Bhutto did not budge during the Calcutta round. In sharp exchanges between American and Pakistani diplomats, the Americans warned that if the negotiations failed because of Pakistan's inflexibility, the international community was likely to accept the status quo on Kashmir.[27] While willing to agree to the cease-fire line as the boundary north and south of the Srinagar Valley, the Pakistanis insisted on some form of plebiscite to determine the ultimate fate of the Valley. In the end, both they and the Indians rejected a U.S.-U.K. suggestion to partition the Valley.[28]

Although by this time President Kennedy had grown increasingly pessimistic about the negotiations, he approved putting forward a joint U.S.-U.K. proposal suggesting "elements of a settlement." This called for what amounted to a "soft border" in the Srinagar Valley, which fudged the issue of sovereignty, and urged a "substantial position in the Vale" for both countries. (See appendix 2 for text of "Elements of a Settlement.")[29] When a bureaucratic mix-up allowed the Pakistanis to receive the elements document before the Indians, Prime Minister Nehru used this as an excuse to finish "these ill-considered and ill-conceived initiatives however well-intentioned they may be . . ." Galbraith cabled that Nehru would have found some escape route other than the "elements" paper as he "is unquestionably angry, in part at my pressure, much more at the fact that I have translated his vague talk of wanting a [Kashmir] settlement into firm concessions that he [Nehru] doesn't want to make."[30]

The negotiations were effectively over even though they dragged on for two more unproductive rounds. In the fifth session, the Pakistanis again chose not to improve their territorial offer. The sixth and final round was a mere formality that took place largely because neither side wanted the talks to end before U.S. Secretary of State Dean Rusk and Commonwealth Secretary Duncan Sandys took their planned visit to South Asia.

The 1962–63 Kashmir negotiations failed for precisely the reasons that U.S. diplomat Averell Harriman had anticipated. Neither India nor Pakistan was willing to make an offer that the other would consider a basis for serious discussion. Their bottom-line positions in the following list remained too far apart for either side to consider a possible compromise.

❖ Both countries were interested in a settlement, but only on their own terms. For Pakistan, this meant some form of self-determination for the people of the Valley; for India, it meant not upsetting the status quo; thus, converting the cease-fire line with minor modifications into an international boundary. Neither side was willing to budge during the talks.

❖ In contrast to the Indus Waters negotiations, the political leadership gave no green light to their negotiators to try to find a way to bridge the gap. For both, talking about a Kashmir settlement was acceptable in response to pressure from the Americans and the British, but making concessions on their respective basic positions was not.

❖ Energetic, sustained, and high-level U.S.-U.K. diplomatic engagement proved fruitless. The efforts to address the Kashmir issue as a technical problem and solve it by drawing lines on a map to divide the disputed Valley, or developing other arrangements, such as a soft border between the two parts of the state, fell on deaf Indian and Pakistani ears.

❖ Despite Pakistan's heavy dependence on U.S. foreign assistance for its economic development and India's relative weakness after the 1962–63 China conflict, neither country was willing to give ground on an issue that each regarded as vital to its national interest in order to please Washington or London.

❖ Even if the leaders had been willing to give ground on Kashmir, neither was politically in a strong position to do so. In Pakistan, political hawks severely criticized Ayub for having failed to take advantage of India's military weakness in order to seize Kashmir by force. In India, Nehru had little scope for making the sort of concessions required to launch a serious Kashmir negotiation, particularly as the China debacle weakened him.

The six rounds of talks in 1962–63 marked the last time that India and Pakistan formally negotiated about a Kashmir settlement. The discussions ultimately went nowhere. As President Kennedy ruefully commented in his September 12, 1963, press conference, "Kashmir is further from being settled today than it was six months ago."[31]

POSTCONFLICT NORMALIZATION NEGOTIATIONS

Tashkent, January 1966

Less than three years later, on January 3, 1966, Indians and Pakistanis gathered for negotiations in the Soviet Central Asian city of Tashkent. The circumstances differed dramatically from the 1962–63 talks. Pakistan's attempt to upset the status quo in Kashmir by force had backfired. Operation Gibraltar, a covert effort to stir an uprising by infiltrating some 8,000 insurgents across the cease-fire line, led to full-scale war. Indian forces struck across the international border in response to a Pakistani armored thrust aimed at cutting off India's road access to the Srinagar Valley. The conflict was short, but nasty. After seventeen days, both sides accepted a UN Security Council call for a cease-fire. Although the two militaries fought to a standoff, India won by not losing.[32]

To Ayub Khan's dismay, President Lyndon Johnson not only refused to help U.S. ally Pakistan, but also cut off economic and military aid, and limited American diplomatic activity to supporting UN peace efforts. In a period of relative détente between Moscow and Washington, the two Cold War rivals cooperated in the Security Council to bring an end to the fighting. After a cease-fire was accepted, the United States supported the Soviet proposal for the two antagonists to use Moscow's good offices to seek a peace settlement.[33]

Both India and Pakistan were not enthusiastic about going to Tashkent, yet neither felt it could refuse Moscow's invitation. India did not want to appear unappreciative for the support the Soviet Union had offered on Kashmir and other issues over the years.[34] Ayub felt constrained to accept the invitation from a country close to India with which Pakistan had had frosty relations.[35] The United States was sitting on the sidelines as Ayub's visit to Washington during December 14–15, 1965, did not yield Lyndon Johnson's support to provide a more active U.S. role. Ayub also found himself in an awkward political position. His government-controlled media had fed the Pakistani public a steady diet of alleged battlefield victories. He needed to come home from Tashkent with something tangible on Kashmir to show that the war had been worthwhile. As the summit neared, Pakistani statements stressed that unless the Tashkent summit addressed the Kashmir issue, the talks had little relevance. At the same time, Ayub privately realized that it was unlikely India would make concessions on Kashmir. During Harriman's visit, Ayub told him, "The Indians are in no mood to be reasonable."[36]

After Nehru died in May 1964, the diminutive, frail, yet tough-minded Lal Bahadur Shastri succeeded him. Prime Minister Shastri and his cabinet colleagues reluctantly concluded that if pressed by the Soviet Union, India would agree to restore the prewar cease-fire line, and to relinquish control of territory it had gained in the fighting. This territory included the strategic Haji Pir Pass, a favored infiltration route across the cease-fire line. The Indians, however, intended to press for Pakistan's agreement on a no-war pact between the two countries, and to refuse to negotiate about Kashmir, as Ayub anticipated. When Shastri publicly floated the idea of the no-war pact, Ayub responded with the typical negative Pakistani reaction to the proposal. Pakistan would agree to such a pact only after, not before, they settled the Kashmir issue.[37]

In order to improve prospects for success at Tashkent, the Soviet Union adopted a more balanced stance on South Asia, showing greater sensitivity to Pakistani concerns, rather than simply echoing Indian positions. To emphasize the importance that Moscow placed on the gathering, Premier Alexei Kosygin led with the assistance of Foreign Minister Andrei Gromyko and Defense Minister Marshall Malinowski. Indian Foreign Minister Swaran Singh and Defense Minister Y.B. Chavan provided support to Prime Minister Shastri. Ayub headed the Pakistani team that included Foreign Minister Z.A. Bhutto and Commerce and Industries Minister Ghulam Faruque.

On January 3, 1966, Shastri and Ayub arrived in Tashkent, listened to Kosygin's warm and identical welcomes, and responded with much diplomatic syrup that they too shared the Soviet leader's desire for peace. Kosygin emphasized the importance of Indian and Pakistani forces' mutual withdrawal to the positions they had held before the fighting began, per the UN Security Council directive. Shastri stressed India's desire for a no-war pact and its unwillingness to discuss Kashmir sovereignty. Ayub declared that he would not agree to a no-war pact until the basic problems separating India and Pakistan were solved. Diplomatically, he did not specifically mention Kashmir as one of the problems.

The conference began with no fixed agenda and the heads of government delegated this task to their subordinates. When Bhutto, Singh, and advisors met, they were unable to agree on what the conference should achieve. Although these discussions continued without positive results, talks between Shastri and Ayub, and their separate meetings with Kosygin became the main diplomatic arena at Tashkent. During his individual sessions with Ayub and Shastri, Kosygin conveyed the gist of his discussions with the other head of government, and passed on his own substantive suggestions on how matters might progress.

The Soviet premier's goal was to fashion an accord that combined the essence of a no-war pact with an agreement on the mutual withdrawal of forces to their prewar positions. When Shastri refused to establish a mechanism to address the Kashmir dispute, Ayub balked. As the talks dragged on, it began to look as if the summit would end without agreement. The anxious Soviets desperately sought a formula to bridge the gap between the Indian and Pakistani positions. On January 9–10, 1966, Kosygin spent an astounding eleven and a half hours in separate and intense discussions with Ayub and Shastri, ending his dogged search for a compromise only at 1:30 A.M.

With the two leaders scheduled to leave Tashkent the next day, there was scant time for the Soviet premier to avert an embarrassing diplomatic failure. Finally, Kosygin's frenetic efforts succeeded. In the early morning of January 10, 1966, Shastri and Ayub agreed upon a compromise formulation. With a beaming Soviet Premier looking on, the Indian and Pakistani leaders signed the Tashkent Declaration at 4:00 P.M. that afternoon.[38] (See the full text at appendix 3.) The following are the main points of the Declaration. India and Pakistan:

❖ agreed on the need for peaceful relations,

❖ pledged not to use force in resolving their differences (India's desire and Pakistan's unwillingness for a no-war pact were adroitly finessed by reference to their obligations under the UN Charter not to resort to the use of force),

❖ stated that they had discussed Kashmir in the context of the desirability of reducing tensions (enabling Ayub to claim that Kashmir had not been ignored),

❖ agreed that they would withdraw their forces to the positions held before the start of hostilities and would repatriate prisoners of war within forty-five days (the major tangible achievement of the summit), and

❖ agreed to restore diplomatic relations including to normalize economic, trade, and communication links, and "to discourage any propaganda directed against the other country."

After a little more than nine hours, at 1:25 A.M. on January 11, 1966, Shastri woke up complaining of chest pains. India's prime minister was suffering a fatal heart attack. He died seven minutes later. During their talks, Ayub and Shastri developed considerable respect for each other even though they had sharp substantive differences, which they did not try to conceal. One can only speculate whether the course of India-Pakistan relations might have been more positive had the Indian leader not suddenly died, possibly enabling him and Ayub to continue the relationship that they began at Tashkent.

In assessing the Tashkent conference, some major conclusions emerge:

❖ The summit marked a signal success for the Soviet Union. Kosygin's skillful and even-handed diplomacy paid off. Even if there was no progress toward a solution of the Kashmir problem, which Kosygin did not realistically expect, the Soviet leader could be proud of his achievement in restoring a modicum of peace between India and Pakistan.

❖ The Soviets' careful, substantive preparation and Kosygin's sustained personal involvement were among the key reasons for the summit's success. The Soviet leader set realistic goals, and despite difficult negotiations, he was able to obtain Ayub's accord on compromise language. Without third-party help, it is unlikely that the two countries would have been able to reach agreement.

❖ Despite intense media attention, the conferees were able to carry on their discussions in relative calm. The international press was kept at a distance during the talks, which helped facilitate the negotiating process. Indian and Pakistani spokesmen were also careful in their comments to the media to avoid scoring points through competitive and conflicting press statements.

❖ In terms of follow through after Tashkent, the two countries implemented the provisions calling for a withdrawal of forces to their prewar positions, and for the exchange of prisoners of war. This meant that India had to relinquish several militarily strategic areas, including the

Haji Pir pass. They also restored diplomatic relations, but bilateral talks on other issues soon stalled. Delhi and Islamabad failed to make any substantial progress toward implementing the Tashkent Declaration's call for establishment of normal economic and commercial ties.

In sum, although Tashkent achieved its immediate objective of restoring the status quo ante bellum, the agreement did not have a long-term positive impact on India-Pakistan relations. Just five years later, India and Pakistan were once more at war.

The reaction to the Tashkent summit was substantially different in the two countries. In India, although there were grumbles about returning hard-gained and strategically significant Kashmir territory to Pakistan, on the whole, Tashkent won public approval. Shastri's death and India's new Prime Minister Indira Gandhi's prompt support for the accord ensured a positive response in New Delhi. In Pakistan, however, Tashkent went down very badly. Ayub Khan paid a heavy political price for the Declaration. Pakistanis thought their leader had given away too much and gained too little of substance on the Kashmir issue. Disapproval was strongest in West Pakistan, where the public believed government propaganda claims that Pakistani troops had inflicted defeat after defeat on the Indians during the conflict.

Sensing Ayub's vulnerability, Foreign Minister Bhutto, ironically a major promoter of Operation Gibraltar, opportunistically began to voice public doubts about Tashkent, implying that he wanted to walk away rather than sign the Declaration. Disheartened, Ayub further weakened himself politically by failing to counter Bhutto's criticism effectively.[39] Tashkent was an important step on the road that ended ultimately in the Pakistani president's downfall in March 1969.

The Simla Summit, July 1972

If Ayub found himself in a tight corner at Tashkent, Bhutto had an even weaker hand when he met with Prime Minister Indira Gandhi at Simla in July 1972. The cool, 7,000-foot summit in the British Raj's former summer capital came six months after Pakistan's defeat in the December 1971 War. This conflict marked the culmination of the crisis that the Pakistani Army initially triggered with its brutal crackdown on East Pakistani separatists in March 1971. When the fighting stopped, 93,000 outgunned Pakistani forces surrendered to the Indian Army in Dhaka, and East Pakistan became the independent nation of Bangladesh.

The disastrous events in East Pakistan psychologically battered Pakistan. It lost half its population, suffered a humiliating military defeat, and received a torrent of international criticism for its harsh treatment of East Pakistanis. In contrast, India had emerged from the war as the dominant power on the subcontinent. A triumphant Indira Gandhi, whom the *Economist* called the "Empress of India," stood at the peak of her power.[40] She had won a resounding electoral victory in March 1971 polls, and her bold and successful management of the East Pakistan crisis added to her popularity and political luster.

Indira Gandhi and a small circle of advisers—many like her, members of the Kashmiri Brahmin subcaste—hoped that a chastened and shrunken Pakistan would accept the new regional strategic reality of India's predominance. In turn, Pakistan would agree to settle the Kashmir dispute by converting the cease-fire line into an international boundary. Failing that, India sought a formal pledge that Pakistan would attempt to settle disputes bilaterally and no longer try to alter the status quo in Kashmir by the use of force or seek dispute intervention by the United Nations, United States, or any other outsiders. Bhutto's negotiating aims were to regain the territory lost in the war in West Pakistan, to free the prisoners of war, and to seek a more stable relationship with India without giving up Pakistani aspirations in regard to Kashmir.[41] While the Kashmir dispute was not a major element of the 1971 East Pakistan crisis, Bhutto knew that India would press hard for a final settlement on the basis of the status quo, which he was determined to avoid.

In keeping with Indian wishes, the 1972 Simla summit was strictly a bilateral affair. Unlike the 1962–63 Kashmir talks, the Americans and British were not hovering in the corridors, or shadowing the negotiations. Unlike Tashkent, the Russians were not offering good offices. Moreover, Indian and Pakistani officials, not the heads of government, were conducting the bulk of the talks. Bhutto's top foreign policy aide Aziz Ahmed, secretary-general of Pakistan's Ministry of External Affairs, and D.P. Dhar, a key adviser to Gandhi although only head of the Foreign Ministry's Policy Planning staff, led the respective negotiating teams. They spent four grueling days trying to fashion an accord.

Agreement appeared unlikely as the two delegations gathered for the farewell dinner that Bhutto hosted for the Indian Prime Minister on the night of July 2, 1972. The Pakistani leader made it clear that he preferred no accord to one that he felt was not in Pakistan's interests.[42] In a dramatic and unscheduled private post-dinner meeting, failure was averted only after the two leaders succeeded in finding language to paper over their differences. Bhutto accepted that all India-Pakistan disputes should be settled peacefully and bilaterally, but was able to obtain Indira Gandhi's approval for a qualifying phrase that permitted both sides to maintain their basic substantive positions. In diplomatic shorthand, this meant that Pakistan did not have to give up its hopes for Kashmir, even though it had accepted India's demand to deal only bilaterally and peacefully on the issue.[43]

Exactly what transpired in the after-dinner exchange between the two leaders remains a subject of dispute between Indians and Pakistanis. Gandhi informed her delegation that Bhutto had told her that he was willing to settle the Kashmir dispute on the basis of the status quo, but he needed time to gain political acceptance for this back home. According to Simla delegation member Abdul Sattar, later Pakistan's foreign secretary and foreign minister, Bhutto said nothing to this effect to the Pakistani team. Bhutto's daughter, Benazir, who was also at Simla, similarly stated that her father never told her anything along these lines. Benazir Bhutto conceded that he might have said this to Mrs. Gandhi in an effort to salvage the summit. As Bhutto and Mrs. Gandhi met alone, and neither left a written record of their discussions, no one will ever know for certain what happened. In any event, what the Pakistani leader may or may not have said in private is only of historical interest, without political or legal relevance.[44]

Among the principal elements of the Simla Agreement, India agreed to return the 5,139 square miles it had occupied in the former West Pakistan during the war, but kept the small amounts of territory it had gained in Kashmir. (Full text of the Simla Agreement is listed in appendix 4.) The two sides agreed to demarcate their positions on the ground in Kashmir when the shooting stopped on December 17, 1971, and to call this the Line of Control (LOC). Both said that they would respect this line "without prejudice to the recognized position of either side." India refused to release the Pakistani prisoners of war without the consent of Bangladesh. This was unlikely to be forthcoming until Pakistan recognized the new state, a step that Bhutto said he was politically not yet ready to take.

Although Pakistan remained unwilling to accept a no-war pact barring a satisfactory arrangement on Kashmir, and was reluctant to agree to India's demand that it drop efforts to internationalize bilateral differences, Islamabad ultimately conceded this point. New Delhi considered the long-sought agreement from Pakistan to address disputes only bilaterally, the major achievement of the summit. The two sides spoke once more of the importance of solving problems through peaceful means, and they agreed to restore diplomatic relations including resuming trade and communications links and undertaking other steps toward normalization. In addition, the Simla Agreement called for periodic summit meetings and diplomatic discussions looking toward "a durable peace and normalization of relations . . . including a final settlement of Jammu and Kashmir."

Simla has similarities with the Tashkent summit despite the fact that the former was a bilateral negotiation, and the latter involved the active good offices of the Soviet Union.

❖ Both summits essentially achieved the reestablishment of the status quo ante bellum; although at Simla, India retained territory gained in Kashmir and did not agree to the immediate release of prisoners of war.

❖ Both negotiations pledged the establishment of normal relations. As events unfolded, however, neither summit succeeded in moving the India-Pakistan bilateral relationship onto a more positive track.

❖ Both Simla and Tashkent required dexterous diplomacy to find language that would gloss over major substantive differences. Directly or indirectly, these related to the Kashmir issue. Soviet Premier Kosygin's good offices succeeded at Tashkent in convincing Ayub to accept a compromise formula. At Simla, Prime Minister Gandhi's willingness to accept a qualifying phrase that preserved Pakistan's underlying position paved the way for a final accord.

❖ The agreement at Simla to establish the LOC to replace the cease-fire line did not mark a major change, though its physical demarcation on the ground was useful in avoiding disputes about which country controlled specific bits of territory. Nonetheless, the failure to demarcate the Siachen Glacier region in the far North led to another long-standing dispute that has yet to be resolved. After the two countries adopted conflicting interpretations about what the Simla Agreement meant for this area, India physically occupied the forbidding 20,000-foot-high glacier starting in 1984. Sporadic fighting continued there for two decades until a cease-fire took effect in December 2003.

❖ Implementing the Simla accords largely paralleled post-Tashkent developments. There was short-term compliance and long-term failure.

    ✧ India gave back the territory that it agreed to return.

    ✧ With some hiccups and delay, they physically delineated the LOC on the ground.

    ✧ India eventually returned the prisoners of war, although it took another year before most were able to go home. In February 1974, just before Bhutto hosted the summit of the Organization of the Islamic Conference in Lahore, another deal was settled. In return for Pakistan's diplomatic recognition, Bangladesh attended the summit and released 195 prisoners it was threatening to prosecute for war crimes.

    ✧ Beyond reestablishing diplomatic relations, India and Pakistan failed to implement other measures to move the two countries toward more normal relations.

In assessing Simla in July 3, 1972, the *New York Times* editorial page aptly concluded that the accord was flawed, "couched in vague terms that are likely to be interpreted differently by the two sides."[45] Since then, India had stressed the agreement to settle all disputes bilaterally and peacefully. Pakistan has emphasized the loophole that spoke of respecting the LOC "without prejudice to the recognized position of either side."

In India, there was a positive reaction to the summit accord. The Simla Agreement was ratified by the president as called for in the Indian constitution. Indira Gandhi also won a parliamentary vote of approval although this was not legally required. Only subsequently have critics begun to assert that Prime Minister Gandhi should have driven a harder bargain.

A witness to, and partly the reason for, the political problems that the Tashkent Declaration caused, Bhutto was particularly sensitive about ensuring a positive public reception for Simla. On his return to Pakistan, he vociferously praised the accord, declaring, "There's nothing against Pakistan's interest in this agreement." Bhutto emphasized that he had not compromised on the Kashmir issue. His efforts were successful, and the Simla accords won an overwhelming endorsement from Pakistan's National Assembly despite the Islamist parties' criticism. Simla had not changed Bhutto's hard-line views about India, which he made clear when meeting with U.S. Treasury Secretary John Connally on July 6, 1972, just a few days after the summit. Connally reported that Bhutto was "enormously upset about the Indians" whom he said "were going to try to use every device they could, including duplicity, to solve their problems at Pakistan's expense."[46]

"TALKS ABOUT TALKS"

Lahore, February 1999

Two decades later and nine months after India and Pakistan had exploded nuclear devices in May 1998, Indian Prime Minister Atal Bihari Vajpayee met with his Pakistani counterpart, Nawaz Sharif, at Lahore. The summit followed a decade during which India-Pakistan relations had badly deteriorated mainly as a result of Pakistan's support for a bloody insurgency that developed in Indian Kashmir following rigged elections in the state.[47] In one sense, Islamabad's tactics succeeded: Pakistan was able to "pay India back" for the humiliating defeat that it had suffered in the December 1971 War. India had to deploy massive army and paramilitary forces to deal with the uprising. The often harsh response of the security forces further antagonized Kashmiris and tarnished India's international human rights image. Since equipping, training, and providing guidance to Kashmiri militants was inexpensive, support for the insurgency cost the Pakistan treasury relatively little. Although the troubles in Kashmir succeeded with India agreeing to talk about the issue with Pakistan, they did not result in any shift in New Delhi's bedrock refusal to countenance any loss of sovereignty over India's part of the state.

Despite the ongoing insurgency, official talks between India and Pakistan continued in a desultory fashion during the early 1990s. Their prospects improved after India's Foreign and later Prime Minister Inder K. Gujral initiated what he called a good neighbor policy in 1996. This enabled the two foreign secretaries, Najmuddin Sheikh of Pakistan and Salman Haider of India, to work out a framework for comprehensive bilateral talks, called the "composite dialogue." The idea was not to try to solve differences in one comprehensive negotiation, but to break down bilateral problems in discrete "baskets" including Kashmir and to address these in separate, but parallel talks. The formula met Pakistan's desire that Kashmir not be pushed aside and forgotten, and satisfied India's wish that all issues be addressed, not just Kashmir. As the "composite dialogue" began, officials discussed various issues, predictably reiterating their side's standard position and making little progress. Nonetheless, the bilateral atmospherics remained positive during 1997. Gujral and Nawaz Sharif, who became prime minister after Benazir Bhutto was dismissed a second time in November 1996, had positive encounters at a South Asia regional summit in the Maldives and at the United Nations.

Just as hopes for progress rose, domestic Indian politics intervened to stall the dialogue. Gujral's government fell, and new elections in March 1998 brought the Hindu-nationalist Bharatiya Janata Party (BJP) to power in a major political shift. Two months later, in May 1998, India tested its nuclear weapons capability, and Pakistan responded with its own nuclear tests. As India and Pakistan came out of the nuclear closet, their festering bilateral frictions and the ongoing Kashmir insurgency gained vastly more international attention. Major capitals, especially Washington, feared that any outbreak of fighting between the two enemies might escalate, even though unintentionally, into a nuclear conflict.

Although both Nawaz Sharif's Pakistan Muslim League and Atal Bihari Vajpayee's BJP supported a more nationalist and hard-line stance than their main political rivals, respectively the Pakistan Peoples Party and the Indian National Congress, the two leaders personally favored India-Pakistan détente and were willing to risk the ire of hard-liners in trying for better relations. When Sharif suggested that Vajpayee ride the inaugural run of a new biweekly bus service between Delhi and Lahore, the Indian prime minister was quick to accept. On February 20, 1999, less than a year after India and Pakistan rattled nerves around the globe with their nuclear tests, Nawaz Sharif warmly embraced Vajpayee after he clambered down from the bus and walked across the border some fifteen miles from Lahore.

The two-day summit featured a highly publicized reception for Vajpayee at the Governor's House in Lahore, a dinner in his honor at the historic Red Fort built by the Mughal emperors, and a dramatic visit to the Minar-i-Pakistan, the monument at the spot where in March 1940 the League had adopted the resolution calling for Pakistan. The public rhetoric was extremely warm. "My message to the people of Pakistan will be short and simple," Vajpayee declared on entering Pakistani territory, "Put aside the bitterness of the past and let us together make a new beginning."[48] At the Government House reception, Vajpayee commented that history could be altered, but not geography; you could choose your friends but not your neighbors.[49] Several times, Vajpayee stressed that a "strong and stable Pakistan is in India's interest."[50]

For his part, Sharif was equally positive. "The time is not far away when Pakistan and India will be able to live as the United States and Canada do—in peace," he declared in welcoming Vajpayee.[51] During the press conference at the end of the summit, Sharif stated, "Whatever happens in India they blame Pakistan. Whatever happens in Pakistan we blame India. There is a need now of getting out of this . . . neither India nor Pakistan has gained anything from the conflicts and tensions of the past 50 years."[52]

While the political leaders were engaging in high-level and positive symbolism, their subordinates produced the Lahore Declaration. This provided a framework for a renewed bilateral dialogue and offered mutual pledges that the two countries would endeavor to resolve their problems peacefully and constructively. The Declaration included agreement to restart the "composite dialogue" about all issues, including Kashmir, and to initiate a series of nuclear-related discussions and confidence-building measures. (The full text of the Lahore Declaration can be found in appendix 5.)

Detracting from the summit's glow were strident anti-India demonstrations in Lahore by followers of the Jamaat-i-Islami, Pakistan's major Islamist party. To the government's embarrassment, the demonstrators physically roughed up a number of diplomats who were on their way to the official dinner that Sharif was hosting for Vajpayee in Lahore's Mughal Fort.[53] The failure of the Pakistan military service commanders to greet India's prime minister at the border struck another off-key note. Although the service chiefs were welcoming a Chinese military delegation in

Islamabad, their absence suggested that the army leadership was not overly enthused about Sharif's hopes for détente with India. Despite these hiccups, the Lahore summit appeared to be a major success.

❖ On the public relations side, Vajpayee's inaugurating the Lahore-Delhi bus service and his visit to the Minar-i-Pakistan conveyed a powerful message of friendship. Substantively, the agreements to renew the languishing "composite dialogue" and begin a new and separate track on nuclear issues seemed to be similarly positive developments.

❖ India and Pakistan came away with the feeling that each had gained. India received Pakistan's reaffirmation of the Simla Agreement calling for the two countries to address issues peacefully and bilaterally and to seek an ultimate solution of differences. Pakistan got official Indian recognition that Kashmir was an "issue" and a problem that needed to be addressed. The rest of the world was pleased by the agreement, particularly the accord to undertake nuclear confidence-building measures.

❖ In the preparatory work before the summit, senior Indian and Pakistani officials were able to take advantage of ongoing bilateral discussions regarding resumption of the "composite dialogue" and establishment of a nuclear dialogue. These set the stage for a relatively easy agreement during the summit.

❖ To follow up the Lahore Declaration, a secret back channel was established to address the Kashmir problem. With official blessing from the two governments, former Pakistan Foreign Secretary Niaz Naik and Indian political insider R.K. Mishra held a number of secret talks to begin an exploration of what a possible Kashmir settlement might look like.

❖ The fact that the political parties of the two prime ministers were more hard-line and nationalist than the major opposition parties probably made it easier for the two leaders to reach the summit agreement. Neither Vajpayee nor Sharif was vulnerable to criticism for having sold out to the other side. As it turned out, Sharif's problem lay in his failure to gain the wholehearted support of the Pakistan Army leadership. The army feared that India would be willing only to talk about Kashmir, but not seriously try to solve the problem.

The flame of the Lahore summit did not burn for long. It was snuffed out abruptly three months later in the spring of 1999 when the Indians became aware that the Pakistani Army had clandestinely taken advantage of frigid winter weather to occupy strategic heights on the Indian side of the Kashmir LOC near Kargil. From nearly impregnable 15,000-foot-high positions, Pakistani troops, wearing civilian clothes and described as Kashmiri "freedom fighters," could interdict the main Indian road link to Ladakh in northeastern Kashmir.

The discovery of the incursion instantly destroyed the spirit of Lahore. India struck back militarily against the Pakistanis entrenched on the Kargil heights. Alarm bells went off around the globe. The widening of fighting between the two nuclear-armed neighbors seemed possible, but was eventually avoided. Under military pressure from India and political pressure from the United States, Pakistan ultimately agreed to pull back the forces from India's side of the LOC. In a July 4, 1999, meeting with U.S. President Bill Clinton at the White House, Nawaz Sharif agreed to use his influence to bring about the withdrawal of Pakistani fighters from across the LOC.[54]

The Indians felt badly deceived and were in no mood to proceed with either the "composite dialogue," or nuclear confidence-building measures. Back channel discussions were aborted.[55] The October 1999 military coup that brought Chief of Army Staff General Pervez Musharraf to power was another disincentive to resume dialogue. New Delhi regarded Pakistan's new chief as the godfather of the Kargil adventure and a hawk on India.

The Lahore summit ultimately proved to be a successful negotiation, but it was derailed and not implemented because the subsequent Kargil mini-war completely soured the bilateral atmosphere. The process of "composite dialogue" envisaged at the summit was stillborn. The Lahore experience underscored the importance of ensuring that bilateral India-Pakistan undertakings gained the support of all key elements in the power structures. In Pakistan, this meant having the backing of the Pakistan Army leadership, even during the period of democratically elected governments during the 1990s. Sharif's failure to achieve this support doomed his effort at détente.[56]

Agra, July 2001

Although India-Pakistan relations remained in the doldrums for two years following the Kargil adventure, the Vajpayee government announced a cease-fire of offensive military operations in Kashmir in fall 2000. In spite of the refusal of the Kashmiri insurgents to cooperate, Delhi prolonged this for an extended period. When the Vajpayee government decided to end the cease-fire in May 2001, it coupled this with a surprise invitation for Musharraf to visit India in July. This set the stage for what proved to be perhaps the most dramatic, but ultimately most disappointing, India-Pakistan summit.

Fairly extensive consultations among senior officials had preceded previous parlays, but not in the case of Agra. Although the two sides held some preliminary talks, Pakistan was reluctant to enter into detailed discussions. There was agreement regarding the schedule; however, no meeting of the minds occurred on substantive goals.[57] India's public statements indicated Delhi's interest in resuming the Lahore summit dialogue, and in obtaining Islamabad's agreement to phase out its support for the Kashmir insurgency. Pakistani statements focused on the importance of tackling the Kashmir issue. This was consistent with the view, which the army leadership strongly held, that failure to make progress on this "core" issue would render illusory progress achieved on other India-Pakistan problems.

Musharraf accepted the invitation and soon after appointed himself president (previously he was called the chief executive officer). He arrived in New Delhi amid enormous public excitement on July 15, 2001. The emotional high point of the day came when Musharraf returned to the house located in the heart of Old Delhi from which his family had fled in August 1947 when he was four years old. Indian President K.R. Narayanan hosted a state dinner with Musharraf as the guest of honor, and he was the first Pakistani leader to lay a wreath at the memorial to Mahatma Gandhi along the banks of the Jumna River. He had a one-on-one meeting with Prime Minister Vajpayee. During this session, the Indian leader accepted Musharraf's invitation to pay a return visit to Pakistan to initiate what many assumed would be a series of regular summit meetings. The day's only sour note was Indian officials' boycott of a reception that Ashraf Qazi, Pakistan high commissioner, hosted as he invited a number of Kashmiri separatists.[58]

The contrast between Vajpayee and Musharraf was striking. The aging Vajpayee was slow afoot, shuffling rather than walking with the help of two artificial knees. He spoke hesitantly and softly in English, though an eloquent orator and poet in Hindi. Known for his long pauses, Vajpayee often seemed distant in conversations. Although a member of the BJP's hardline Rashtriya Swayamsevak Sangh (RSS), or national volunteer organization, the prime minister was a political moderate who had long advocated peaceful and friendly relations with Pakistan. In contrast, the fifty-seven-year-old Musharraf walked briskly like the paratrooper and commando he had been, wore a ramrod military bearing, and spoke often, quickly, and bluntly. The Pakistani leader made little effort to hide his strong feelings about India and his open support for the Kashmir insurgency.

The following day, the summit shifted to Agra where the two delegations were housed in adjacent luxury hotels. While Vajpayee and Musharraf had a second meeting alone, their foreign ministers and staffs were frenetically trying to fashion a joint statement that would relaunch the bilateral dialogue. The going was slow as draft texts passed back and forth between the delegations during the day and evening. The sticking point centered on Kashmir. Pakistan wanted the issue underscored as the key dispute that needed addressing. India was ready to acknowledge the importance of Kashmir, but also wanted Pakistan to agree to reduce its unacknowledged support for the insurgency. That evening, breaking a tacit understanding about dealing with the press, the Indian Information and Broadcasting Minister Sushma Swaraj upset the Pakistanis by suggesting that the two leaders had talked about a wide variety of subjects, but not about Kashmir. The Pakistanis promptly countered that Kashmir had been front and center in the discussions.[59]

The morning of July 17, 2001, the Pakistani president had a breakfast meeting with Indian editors in what was supposedly an off-the-record session. Cameras were present, however, and Pakistani and one Indian television channel aired his remarks live. At his most open, Musharraf spoke frankly and with much emotion about India-Pakistan differences. He made clear his strong feelings about Kashmir, comparing this issue to the Palestinian struggle with Israel. Pakistan's President reiterated that progress on other bilateral matters was possible only in parallel with progress on Kashmir.[60]

Musharraf was great copy and gripping television, but by going public, whether or not planned, he incensed the Indian leadership, which was then meeting to consider how best to respond to the latest draft of the communiqué. In reaction to what they regarded as Musharraf's breach of diplomatic practice, the Indians dug in their heels. The Pakistani leader was supposed to leave Agra that afternoon to visit the shrine of a Muslim saint in Ajmer, but he postponed his departure to permit more time to continue the frantic search for common language. That evening, Musharraf gave up and decided to return to Pakistan. Before departing, he paid a farewell call on Vajpayee that lasted ninety minutes. Around midnight, the Pakistani leader left Agra and returned to Islamabad. There was neither a joint statement nor a press conference. A summit that had begun with high hopes ended in mutual recriminations.[61]

In the ensuing blame game, the Pakistanis claimed that the Indians agreed to a joint statement and then backed off. Although Vajpayee, they asserted, was willing to accept the draft the two foreign ministers developed, Home Minister L.K. Advani and other cabinet hawks supposedly overruled him. Trying to put the best face on the summit failure, Pakistan's Foreign Minister Abdul Sattar commented that the two sides had evolved a process to promote the bilateral dialogue, and they could build on this achievement in subsequent talks. Nirupama Rao, the Indian Foreign Ministry spokesperson, responded coolly that the starting point for India would not be steps discussed at Agra, but rather the accords reached at Lahore and Simla. Since India and Pakistan did not reach a final agreement at Agra, Rao stated that the two sides would have to begin any future talks *de novo.*[62]

Vajpayee failed to win the public relations battle and the opposition Congress party and elements of his own BJP criticized him for supposedly having bungled the summit. In response, Vajpayee lashed back sharply at Musharraf. Employing atypical undiplomatic words, Vajpayee called Pakistan's president "quite clueless about our history, politics, and the rules of international diplomacy."[63] In sum, what could explain the unhappy ending of the 2001 summit?

❖ The presummit substantive preparations for the Agra gathering were wholly inadequate. As a result, Vajpayee and Musharraf began the talks without the benefit of preliminary discussions that permitted agreement on most issues. Instead of the summit's focusing on the remaining substantive differences, the fundamentals had still to be tackled.

❖ If at Lahore, Nawaz Sharif failed to gain the wholehearted support of the Pakistan Army leadership, at Agra, Prime Minister Vajpayee had not fully reconciled differences within his ruling coalition before the summit began. In the end, the collective Indian leadership proved unwilling to accept the language of the draft communiqué that Foreign Minister Jaswant Singh, his Pakistani counterpart Abdul Sattar, and their aides developed.

❖ At Tashkent, Simla, and Lahore, the actual negotiations were conducted largely in private until the two sides neared closure. Not so at Agra. The media hoopla surrounding the Agra summit doubtlessly impaired the prospects for success. Neither side followed tacitly understood, if not explicitly agreed upon, ground rules for dealing with the media. In earlier summits, the press, which an official spokesperson carefully spoon-fed, was generally kept at arm's length. At Agra, both sides violated these implicit rules.

❖ Public diplomacy was a major and positive element during the Lahore summit, and the good publicity benefited both sides. During the Agra summit, however, Musharraf was far more visible, vocal, and newsworthy than Vajpayee. This was due partly to the novelty of the Pakistani leader's visiting his childhood home and to his outgoing and media-friendly public style. It is hard to escape the conclusion that he was trying to appeal to the people of India by going over the head of its government. In doing so, Musharraf greatly reduced the chances for substantive success.

In the end, the Agra summit proved a major diplomatic failure. Not only were India and Pakistan unable to reach agreement or advance the prospects for détente and dialogue, but the summit's collapse also left the bilateral relationship in worse condition. Given the high expectations and media attention generated during the initial part of Musharraf's visit, the inability of the two leaders to come to closure on a communiqué was deeply depressing in both countries. Indians followed Vajpayee's lead in blaming Musharraf for showboating, and the Pakistanis blamed BJP hardliners for torpedoing the final draft. Since the Agra summit ended in shambles and without agreement, there was nothing to implement after the summit's collapse.

3

ASSESSING THE INDIA-PAKISTAN NEGOTIATING EXPERIENCE

NEGOTIATING PATTERNS

Although a variety of events and circumstances triggered the negotiations examined in this study, the underlying theme is the search for more normal India-Pakistan relations. Apart from the Canal Waters discussions of the 1950s, all cases touched on the Kashmir problem, despite the 1962–63 talks which were the only dialogue specifically intended to solve this dispute. With the exception of the Waters talks, the substantively barren negotiations have provided little tangible and long-term value. Beyond resolving postconflict issues at Tashkent and Simla and agreeing to a framework for future talks at Lahore, the five negotiations ultimately rendered futile diplomatic exercises.

Although there are many ways of examining and comparing negotiations, Professor Raymond Cohen has developed one of the more useful analytical approaches in his pioneering study, *Negotiating Across Cultures*.[64] This study employs a variant of his approach. Cohen parses different stages of negotiations in terms of the run-up, the opening and middle phases, a crisis point ending in either deadlock or breakthrough, and, assuming agreement is reached, the implementation phase. In addition to these stages, this study includes three additional elements: the role of the media, the involvement of external players, and the impact of cultural differences on the negotiations.

The Run-Up to Negotiations

Preliminary discussions have preceded formal India-Pakistan negotiating sessions, usually conducted by senior-level officials. These premeeting discussions were preferably conducted in private, away from the glare of media. These preliminary talks have played an important role in setting the scene and laying out the scope, parameters, and likely directions of subsequent negotiations. Good preparatory work has been a precondition for a successful outcome. At Simla and Lahore, preliminary talks set the stage for positive summits. Even so, adequate preparations have not in themselves ensured success; witness the failure of the 1962–63 Kashmir talks. A lack of sufficient preparation, however, almost certainly leads to an unsuccessful outcome. The inadequate presummit deliberations in 2001 were a significant factor in the ultimate failure of the Agra summit.

The Negotiations Get Underway: Discovering the Differences

After the opening formalities and official greetings for the visiting side (or in Tashkent, both visiting sides), formal business would begin. Except for Tashkent, the heads of government generally have not dealt with the substantive nuts and bolts, and left these in the hands of subordinates. At some point in the discussions, the major sticking points between the two sides become clear. One or more key issues usually emerge as the critical point of bargaining and negotiation. Sometimes, it has been a search for the right words for the communiqué; at other times, it has involved concrete gestures or actions by one side or the other. Both sides are acutely aware of the negotiating record. Words and phrases in various statements and communiqués have acquired highly specific meanings. Budging from favored and traditionally held formulations has proven excruciatingly difficult for either side.

❖ In the Indus Waters talks, the key issues were finding a formula to share the Canal Waters and the means to pay for new construction.

❖ In the 1962–63 Kashmir talks, after the initial exchanges agreed on establishing an international boundary, the challenge was to find a way to achieve this in a mutually acceptable manner.

❖ At Tashkent, Ayub's desire to show that he had achieved something on Kashmir, and India's desire for a no-war pact were the two principal negotiating challenges.

❖ At Simla, the negotiations turned on Indira Gandhi's desire to obtain Pakistan's agreement to settle all disputes bilaterally and no longer involve other powers, and Bhutto's desire not to undercut Pakistan's long-term aspirations for Kashmir.

❖ At Lahore, Pakistan wanted to gain acceptance for its position that Kashmir be regarded as the core bilateral problem. This was also a central issue at Agra where India wanted Pakistan to agree that it would curb support for the Kashmir insurgency.

The Crisis Point: Breakthrough or Breakdown

At some point, negotiations normally reach an impasse. Much has been agreed upon, but one or another key substantive issue or important point in the draft communiqué or statement remains in dispute. In summits involving heads of government, pressure quickly mounts. They have busy schedules, and cannot extend their stays by any appreciable period. Failure now seems a possibility, if not a probability. The leaders must decide whether to accept a breakdown, or to make a concession that enables a breakthrough.

❖ In the Canal Waters negotiations, conducted over a number of years by senior civil servants and not the heads of government, intense time pressure was absent. Lengthy consultations back at the national capitals followed the negotiating sessions. When the two sides reached an impasse over the principles for water sharing, the World Bank broke the deadlock with its own proposals. Six years of highly detailed and technical negotiations were then required to reach final agreement.

❖ In the 1962–63 Kashmir talks, both sides had to decide whether to make concessions that they did not want to make in order to permit serious bargaining toward a settlement of the dispute. When they refused to do so, the negotiations failed.

❖ At Tashkent, Ayub swallowed hard and accepted a Soviet compromise formula that gave him little to show on Kashmir beyond that the subject was discussed during the talks.

❖ At Simla, Indira Gandhi avoided a breakdown by agreeing in the post-dinner private meeting with Bhutto to a verbal formula that enabled the Pakistani leader to avoid making concessions that he did not want to make.

❖ At Lahore, the negotiations, on the whole, went smoothly. Presummit discussions regarding nuclear confidence-building measures and the composite dialogue made it possible to reach an agreement with relative ease.

❖ At Agra, after the two sides could not find mutually acceptable communiqué language to deal with the related issues of Kashmir and Pakistan's support for the insurgency, the summit collapsed.

Implementation

Indians and Pakistanis have generally implemented specific actions that they agreed upon during the negotiations. They have not implemented, however, less tangible, longer-term goals, such as achieving normal political and economic relations and settling all bilateral disputes, including Kashmir.

❖ The most impressive negotiating success remains the 1960 Canal Waters agreement. The treaty is still intact four decades after the signing, despite the many stresses and strains of India-Pakistan relations. So far, both sides have implemented the treaty provisions in dealing with problems. Currently, Pakistan's claim that the Baglihar power project violates the treaty provisions triggered a dispute that has come to a head. A World Bank-appointed neutral observer is presently studying the issue. The expert's finding will once more test the agreement's stability.

❖ In the unsuccessful 1962–1963 Kashmir talks, no agreement was reached, leaving nothing to implement.

❖ At Tashkent and Simla, the two countries implemented the specific short-term measures agreed upon during the summits, namely to return territory, to exchange prisoners (Tashkent), and to reopen diplomatic missions. They failed, however, to implement longer-term measures, most importantly, launching and sustaining an effort to normalize relations. Once they achieved the status quo ante bellum, India and Pakistan resumed their default mode of chronic friction.

❖ At Lahore, the agreement became a dead letter after the Kargil crisis. Neither nuclear confidence-building measures nor the "composite dialogue" materialized. The secret back channel was shut down.

❖ At Agra, as the parties failed to reach agreement, there was nothing to implement.

The Media and Public Opinion

The public relations aspects of the summits have always been important—Ayub's problems at Tashkent, for example—and in recent years these have at times overshadowed the substantive negotiations. At Lahore, Vajpayee's visit to the Minar-i-Pakistan conveyed a powerful and politically positive message of India's acceptance of Pakistan for millions of television viewers. Similarly, Musharraf's emotionally charged return to his boyhood home caught the imagination of millions of Indian and Pakistani viewers; whereas, his controversial breakfast remarks on television impaired the prospects for agreement.

Before the start of any diplomatic negotiation, senior leaders' statements at press briefings and in public are extremely important. They establish the tone for the upcoming negotiations, signal the likely areas of contention, and articulate the public goals of the two sides. Indian and Pakistani spokesmen have to be careful that their statements addressing various domestic constituencies do not roil the waters for the meetings. At times, both sides have violated the golden rule of "no surprises" in public announcements and statements that touch on the upcoming negotiations. One country's comments have often caused negative responses from the other, impairing the prospects for the talks. For example, Nehru's comments that any change in the status of Kashmir would be a bad thing nearly scuttled the 1962–63 negotiations before they began. In 2001, Musharraf's going over the head of the Indian government by trying to appeal directly to the Indian public on television clearly impaired the prospects for agreement at Agra.

Until recent years, newspaper and television coverage on the whole has faithfully reflected the respective official lines. Government spokespersons in both countries typically spoon-fed the media regarding the negotiation status. Since the advent of a freer press in Pakistan in the late 1980s and of satellite television in the 1990s, this situation has changed, and coverage has become more nuanced. Indian and Pakistani citizens have been receiving a much wider range of information than previously. Television viewers have access to numerous channels outside of direct government control, including several twenty-four-hour news stations. As the press has become more independent, it no longer echoes official positions.

Third Party Involvement

In the Canal Waters negotiations, the 1962–63 Kashmir talks, and the 1966 Tashkent summit, the World Bank, U.S.-U.K., and Soviet officials were actively engaged in the negotiations, albeit in different ways. In the Waters negotiations and Tashkent, respectively the World Bank and the Soviets were direct parties to the talks. In 1962–1963, the Americans and the British were diplomatically engaged, but not physically present in negotiating sessions. Since Tashkent, Indians and Pakistanis have negotiated with each other without direct outsider involvement.

Traditionally, Pakistan has eagerly sought third party involvement; whereas India has strongly preferred to deal bilaterally with its neighbor. From the Indian perspective, the experience with UN and then American and British engagement regarding Kashmir in the late 1940s, 1950s, and early 1960s proved unsatisfactory. For various reasons, mainly Cold War alliance considerations, New Delhi believed that outsiders opposed the Indian position and favored the Pakistani stance on Kashmir. India has since been firmly against anything more than third party diplomatic facilitation, and has often been reluctant to accept even that involvement. New Delhi regarded Pakistan's agreement at Simla in 1972—that it would no longer seek to internationalize India-Pakistan problems, but would deal with them only bilaterally—as a major achievement.

In contrast, and as the weaker party, Pakistan has actively sought to involve other countries as a way of offsetting India's greater strength. In the 1940s and 1950s, when there was considerable international support for a Kashmir plebiscite, the Pakistanis were correct in judging that external involvement worked to their advantage. Since the two nations conducted nuclear tests in 1998 and the war on terrorism began in September 2001, this is no longer the case. The primary concern in capitals outside South Asia, especially in Washington, is to reduce the threat of conflict between the two countries, rather than to address the substance of the Kashmir dispute. During the Kargil crisis in 1999, President Bill Clinton pressed Prime Minister Nawaz Sharif to withdraw Pakistani forces from the Indian side of the LOC in order to reestablish the status quo. U.S. intervention, in effect, favored India's position, not Pakistan's. Similarly, during the 2002–03 crisis, the Bush administration and other governments pressed Pakistan to do everything possible to stop infiltration of insurgents across the LOC. Again, external involvement served India's interests, rather than Pakistan's.

Neither Islamabad nor New Delhi seems to have fully factored the shift of foreign attitudes into its thinking. Pakistan continues to solicit outsiders' engagement despite the fact that this is no longer likely to be to its advantage. New Delhi remains allergic to active external engagement in India-Pakistan problems, even though outsiders are unlikely to support a change in the status quo.[65]

The Significance of Cultural Differences

In *Negotiating Across Cultures*, Raymond Cohen provides numerous illustrations where cultural differences caused major negotiating problems, which led to serious misunderstandings. In the case of India and Pakistan, however, it is hard to argue convincingly that this has happened. Cultural distinctions and different negotiating styles indeed have not been a significant factor in their parlays. It is true that the Pakistani state has developed a substantial Islamist flavor, especially in the years since General Zia-ul Haq took power in 1977; and the BJP-led government emphasized India's Hindu roots during its six years in power (1998–2004). Nonetheless, fifty years after partition, the national security and diplomatic establishments in Islamabad and Delhi—the officials who actually conduct the negotiations—continue to look very much alike. Both remain chips off the British block.

Members of Indian and Pakistani negotiating teams disagree sharply on the substantive issues, but they are usually quite amicable on a personal basis, and interact easily at social gatherings. In conducting negotiations, team members converse in English with intermittent use of Hindi-Urdu, the lingua franca of Pakistan and much of India. All written communications and documents between the two sides are in English. Indian and Pakistani diplomats do not face linguistic difficulties of the sort that may occur when the two sides speak different languages requiring interpreters to translate what each other is saying.

In their negotiations, Indians and Pakistanis have no problem in understanding the perspective of their interlocutor. Indian and Pakistani diplomats have spent their careers working on bilateral relations, and know the record virtually by heart. They possess a detailed understanding of the substantive positions that the other has taken in the past, even if they often have conflicting and intuitionally frozen interpretations of the other side's actions and intentions. Indian and Pakistani negotiators fully comprehend the implications of each other's body language, and other cultural South Asian mannerisms. Cultural misunderstandings have not been the stumbling block in India-Pakistan negotiations; the obstacle has been the substantive gap between the two countries and their great reluctance to compromise even on relatively small points.

As noted earlier, the major institutional difference between the two countries lies in the fact that the Pakistan Army dominates policymaking in Islamabad; whereas, in New Delhi power lies in the hands of a civilian Prime Minister chosen by the popularly elected *Lok Sabha*. In Pakistan, as the Lahore summit showed, no significant bilateral understanding with India is likely to prove durable unless the army leadership gives them full assent. Although the Islamist parties may vehemently oppose détente with India, it would be noisy, but not decisive, given the army's support for détente.

In India, coalition governments have ruled in New Delhi since the emergence of the BJP as a second major national party in the 1990s. This situation, which differs from the era of Congress party domination, means that support from the major opposition party has become a necessary underpinning for any major agreement with Pakistan. As the opposition, the BJP can be expected to criticize specific aspects of negotiations; however, the party is likely to support agreements that fall within the broad parameters of the approach the Vajpayee government adopted.

PAST FAILURES HAVE BEEN PROLOGUE

For more than half a century after Britain transferred power, India and Pakistan have remained trapped in history. They have shown little proclivity to move very far beyond emotionally charged differences that resulted in partition and the traumatic and tragic events of 1947. The legacy of distrust and suspicion has weighed heavily on their bilateral relations, with subsequent friction, including three wars and the Kargil crisis that reinforced initial enmity and mistrust. Under these discouraging circumstances, their inability to negotiate a settlement of the Kashmir dispute and to bridge other differences has hardly been surprising. With the exception of the

Canal Waters Treaty of 1960, itself an eight-year marathon, India and Pakistan have failed in the major negotiations discussed to achieve significant progress toward more normal relations, or even to sustain a negotiating process with this objective.

In the past, both countries' sharp, unflattering, and stereotyped perceptions of each other was a major problem. A negative view of India is especially strong in Pakistan's Army leadership, the country's most influential policymaking institution. As Stephen Cohen points out in his book titled *The Idea of Pakistan* (Washington: Brookings Institution Press, 2004), the Pakistan Army is imbued with the firm belief that India and Hindus are inherently hostile to Pakistan and they seek to weaken the country in every possible way.[66] The rise of the BJP in the late 1990s and the anti-Muslim pogrom in Gujarat in 2002 strengthened these attitudes. In India, the opinion-making elite, including active and retired senior civil servants, diplomats, journalists, military officers, and intelligence officials, has held a highly negative view of Pakistan. Islamabad's support for the Kashmir insurgency and the rise of Islamist extremism in Pakistan deepened Indian concerns about Pakistan.

In bilateral negotiations, particularly in regard to Kashmir, Pakistan has been and continues to be the revisionist power seeking to alter the status quo. India has basically been satisfied with the territorial situation on the ground. Unofficially, India has long been willing to settle the dispute by transforming the cease-fire line and then the LOC into a permanent international border. Although Islamabad in recent years has accepted the idea of the "composite dialogue" as a satisfactory framework for negotiations, it has stressed the importance of moving forward to settle the Kashmir dispute. Musharraf and his predecessors have generally tied normalizing any facet of India-Pakistan relations to progress on Kashmir. The Pakistanis have feared that if they allow relations to improve in such areas as trade and commerce, the Indians would simply pocket any Pakistani concessions, and not seriously consider changing the Kashmir status quo. As one top-level Pakistani official averred, "We are the weaker party. What else do we have as a bargaining card in dealing with India?"[67]

In approaching discussions with Pakistan, India has preferred to start with less tendentious issues, and put Kashmir on a back burner. New Delhi would like to follow the negotiating strategy that it and Beijing have adopted in addressing their bilateral problems. This is to focus first on questions like normalization of economic ties and postpone more intractable problems, such as the long-disputed India-China border. In dealing with Pakistan, India is willing to have the "composite dialogue" including Kashmir as one of the baskets, but does not believe it is useful to seek a solution in the short-term.

Up to a point, this approach is valid. Agreements on the easier problems (for example, the dispute over Siachen Glacier) would gradually lead to an improvement in the overall India-Pakistan atmosphere, help reduce mutual mistrust, develop a greater level of confidence in the bona fides of the other side, and make it possible for the two countries eventually to make constructive progress with Kashmir. The weakness in the Indian argument, however, is that New Delhi has been sluggish in paying adequate attention to a key element of the Kashmir problem—New Delhi's heavy-handed governance that alienates Kashmiris in the Srinagar Valley. Islamabad has played a significant role in fanning the flames of Kashmir insurgency, but discontent has been fundamentally homegrown. There are some recent signs of greater Indian flexibility, specifically, the willingness to allow dissident Kashmiri leaders to visit Pakistan, and the subsequent meeting between them and Indian Prime Minister Manmohan Singh.

There has also been a historical dimension in Pakistan's strategy that echoes the approach that Jinnah successfully adopted in the negotiations regarding India's future in the decade between 1937 and 1947. In parlays with the Congress and the British, the Muslim League chief tenaciously pursued the goal of Pakistan, showing total inflexibility on the issue even though many doubted that the two-nation concept, whatever its theoretical validity, was practical. With similar single-mindedness, Pakistan has fixed on solving the Kashmir issue as a fundamental foreign and national security policy objective, and has been willing to subordinate all other aspects of relations with India to this goal. The reasoning is that if Jinnah succeeded in achieving this seemingly impossible dream by persevering and staying the course, why cannot Pakistan attain its goal in Kashmir by demonstrating a similar steadfastness?

DOES PAST REMAIN PROLOGUE?

The current thaw and normalization effort began in the spring of 2003 after Prime Minister Vajpayee called for another attempt to resolve India-Pakistan differences. Over the following six months, secret back channel discussions between Brajesh Mishra, India's national security adviser, and Tariq Aziz, Musharraf's key confidant, set the stage for the start of negotiations. Their talks satisfied both sides with Pakistan seriously attempting to stop jihadi infiltration across the LOC, and India seriously preparing to address the Kashmir dispute as part of the "composite dialogue." In December 2003, in a highly significant development, the guns fell silent in Kashmir. A cease-fire took effect along the LOC and in Siachen, the latter for the first time in two decades. Musharraf and Vajpayee met at the South Asia Association Regional Cooperation (SAARC) summit on January 5, 2004. Follow-on discussions a month later between the two foreign secretaries ended in formal agreement on the modalities and time-table for restarting the "composite dialogue." They agreed to use the framework agreed upon in 1998 and reaffirmed at the February 1999 Lahore summit.

The eight "baskets" in the dialogue range from relatively minor questions, such as the Wular barrage (a decade-old dispute whether an Indian project to improve dry season navigation on the Jhelum River in Kashmir violates the Indus Treaty) and Sir Creek (a dispute over the maritime boundary in the Arabian Sea), to more important issues, such as the Siachen Glacier and a series of much broader and far-reaching policy subjects: terrorism and drug trafficking, economic and commercial cooperation, peace and security, promotion of friendly exchanges in various fields, as well as Kashmir as its own basket.[68]

Although the dialogue was interrupted for a time while the Indian National Congress-led coalition unexpectedly defeated the BJP and its partners in May 2004 general elections and then settled into office, the talks under the different baskets have proceeded apace. By the end of 2005, two full rounds had been completed. Senior civil servants have generally led delegations, but at times ministers were in charge. Periodically, there have been higher-level discussions involving foreign secretaries and foreign ministers to assess overall progress and to provide fresh negotiating impulses. Musharraf, Vajpayee, and Manmohan Singh have met several times, most recently a four-hour session during the annual UN General Assembly meeting in New York in September 2005.

All in all, the "composite dialogue" has marked a positive departure from the past negotiating experience. India and Pakistan have succeeded in establishing and sustaining, for two years at least, a structured dialogue with parallel, but separate talks on various issues aimed at step-by-step normalization. In itself, this development marks a signal step forward, which is something that India and Pakistan had been unable to achieve previously. The two sides have so far not repeated many of the missteps of previous negotiations. There have been adequate and private preparations for top-level meetings, usually through back channels out of public view. Despite Musharraf's occasional slips, the two sides have generally avoided negotiating through the media.

The "composite dialogue" framework has permitted multilayered negotiations on a far wider range of issues than previous summit gatherings. The framework has also reduced pressure for immediate successes. When impasses have been reached, as they have been on many topics, the issues are either put aside for the time being or taken up at a higher level. The broad-gauged dialogue has established a web of intergovernmental contacts that did not previously exist. Indian and Pakistani officials have been slowly learning to work together in addressing problems more constructively. In the process, mutual confidence has grown, and the tendency to automatically doubt the bona fides of the other side has somewhat diminished.

The fact that stakeholders for better relations have become stronger in both countries has reinforced and buttressed the dialogue. Since détente began, political, business, and cultural delegation visits have surged. The wildly successful cricket series in March 2004 that Pakistan hosted marked a psychological high point. In Lahore, Pakistani fans cheered India when it defeated the home side instead of rioting. This signaled quite vividly that public opinion is shifting in favor of finding some way to achieve less hostile relations.

In this context, Indian opinion-makers speak increasingly of the desirability of solving differences with Pakistan, including Kashmir, to facilitate their country's attaining global status as a great power. Senior Pakistanis increasingly assert that their country needs reduced tensions with India in order to make genuine progress in addressing its grave domestic economic and social ailments. Indian and Pakistani political leaders, including Musharraf, have seconded the importance of improved relations with growing intensity. On the Pakistani side, old shibboleths like the need for a Kashmir plebiscite, have been discarded and there is less insistence on conditioning progress in economic and other areas on advances toward a Kashmir settlement.

Notwithstanding genuinely improved bilateral atmospherics and the continuing cease-fire in Kashmir, the tangible negotiating accomplishments have been relatively modest. Under the "peace and security" basket, several confidence-building measures have been announced, such as prior notification regarding missile testing and establishment of new hotlines. The Indian Consulate in Karachi and the Pakistani Consulate in Mumbai are to be reopened. On the travel side, there have also been agreements to reopen rail and road service in a number of places. The most dramatic of these was the February 2005 agreement to resume bus service between Srinagar and Muzaffarabad, linking the capitals of India and Pakistan's parts of Kashmir after a fifty-year lapse.

In practical terms, the accord to have biweekly service is not earthshaking, but it has great symbolic importance, as it enables Kashmiris to travel between these two cities for the first time since the 1947–48 war split the then princely state. The Kashmir bus accord also showed that India and Pakistan had the political will to find ways to compromise on a tough issue. The bus service talks had stalled over the nature of the travel documents. India wanted to require passports, at which Pakistan balked as this would imply recognition of Kashmiris as Indian citizens, thereby undercutting a fundamental Pakistani position that Kashmir was disputed territory and not part of India. Instead of allowing the impasse to become a deadlock, private discussions between Tariq Aziz and the late J.N. Dixit, then Manmohan Singh's national security adviser, succeeded in developing a mutually satisfactory formula: the issuance of special travel documents. To ensure total clarity and understanding regarding the agreement, India's Foreign Minister Natwar Singh personally reviewed the text with President Pervez Musharraf before announcing the accord.[69]

Recent Developments

The catastrophic October 2005 earthquake that devastated the area around Muzaffarabad, killing about 80,000 people and leaving several million homeless, led to a further easing of LOC restrictions. Delhi and Islamabad agreed to open a number of checkpoints to permit the flow of relief goods and possibly some movement of people. The tragic episode, however, underscored continuing sensitivities and rigidities on both sides. Musharraf rejected India's offer of relief helicopters if flown by Indian pilots. The Indians rebuffed Musharraf's call for a broader opening of the LOC out of concern that Islamic militants would cross into India's part of Kashmir.

Another possible step forward, one that could have enormous economic and political consequences, involves a pipeline to transport Iranian natural gas across Pakistan to energy-hungry India. Pakistan, which would stand to gain substantial royalties, has been a strong proponent of the project. Although the BJP-led Indian government had been unwilling to pursue the proposal lest India become dependent on Pakistan for fuel supplies that could be cut off in times of tension, the Congress-led coalition changed the Indian position. It saw the pipeline as not only a source of badly needed energy supplies, but also a means of promoting economic cooperation with Pakistan.

The project is far from becoming a reality. Many technical hurdles must be overcome, such as securing financing and settling complex security arrangements. To complicate matters, the United States, notwithstanding its long-standing support for improved India-Pakistan relations, is opposing the project as part of U.S. efforts to pressure Iran on nonproliferation and other issues. Despite Washington's stance, India and Pakistan are likely to implement the project if other obstacles can be overcome.

While the pipeline will require protracted talks and complicated negotiations, settlement of the Siachen Glacier dispute is a more immediate possibility. Before the November 2003 cease-fire, India and Pakistan had engaged in two decades of expensive, high-altitude warfare over the 20,000-foot-high glacier. Bitterly cold weather caused far more casualties than enemy fire. Talks within the "composite dialogue" framework have so far failed to work out the modalities of a pullback of forces from the disputed area. At their October 2005 meeting, Foreign Ministers Khurshid M.

Kasuri of Pakistan and K. Natwar Singh of India urged the negotiating teams to try to find a solution in the upcoming round of talks. (India and Pakistan came close to solving Siachen a decade ago.) Provided there is political push from the top, officials should be able to develop a mutually acceptable compromise. Their success or failure to do so will provide an indication of the extent to which the two countries can continue the normalization process. Although not a formal part of the "composite dialogue," the dispute over the Baglihar Dam will be another test for the process, as well as for the stability of the Indus Waters Treaty. India will face hard choices if the World Bank expert finds that Pakistan's complaint is justified. If the Indian view is accepted, Pakistan can do little more than grumble.

Despite substantial improvement in relations, underscored by the Manmohan Singh-Musharraf statement after their April 2005 meeting that "the peace process was now irreversible,"[70] it remains unclear how far New Delhi or Islamabad will be able to go in the current normalization effort. Although both governments are rhetorically committed to "a unified negotiating stance for peace," [71] as retired Indian Admiral Verghese Koithara described in *Crafting Peace in Kashmir* (New Delhi: Sage Publications, 2004), it is uncertain if the rhetoric will be translated in reality. By sustaining the "composite dialogue" for a considerable time period, India and Pakistan have built the foundation for gradual and step-by-step agreements on outstanding issues. The momentum is positive, but progress has been very slow. For any number of reasons, the "composite dialogue" can still stall or collapse. As the fate of the Israel-Palestine Oslo Peace Accords sadly shows, no negotiating process is "irreversible" until final agreements are reached and outstanding differences are resolved.

Future Prospects

At present, leaders in New Delhi and Islamabad appear committed to gradual reconciliation and normalization within the agreed negotiating framework. It is essential that both countries continue to maintain this attitude in order to further progress. A number of possible developments, however, can influence how the leaders will regard matters and the affect on prospects (positive or negative) for further normalization. These events could involve the following outcomes:

❖ An intensified movement of people between India and Pakistan could increase public pressures in favor of further reductions in travel restrictions as well as accelerated progress toward normalization.

❖ Growing trade and commerce between the two countries could create important "lobbies" in both capitals advocating normalization. In the past, the absence of significant India-Pakistan economic relations has focused bilateral dealings almost exclusively on intractable political-security issues.

❖ Musharraf himself has launched a discussion inside Pakistan about possible options for a Kashmir settlement. Opinion in India has previously reflected a wider range of options on Kashmir. Greater flexibility in Pakistanis' attitudes would make it easier to make progress toward a Kashmir settlement.

❖ An agreement regarding autonomy for Indian Kashmir between New Delhi and Kashmiri dissidents could have a profound effect on the situation. An accord on autonomy would reduce the pressures on Pakistan to support Kashmiri self-determination and facilitate finding a mutually satisfactory solution.

❖ On the negative side, a Pakistani decision to ignore its commitment to try to prevent jihadi infiltration across the Kashmir LOC would severely damage normalization prospects. Islamist terrorist incidents that New Delhi linked to Islamabad would at the least stall and possibly sink the "composite dialogue." Although the bomb explosions in crowded New Delhi markets in late October 2005 have not derailed the process, another major terrorist incident could.

❖ An upheaval in Pakistan's political leadership that resulted in a larger policy voice for Islamist and other anti-India elements could seriously impair and possibly terminate the negotiations. A similar political development seems less likely in India, but cannot be totally excluded. Presently, both major Indian political parties favor détente with Pakistan. Even though the BJP initiated the détente process when it was in power, the party contains a Hindu fundamentalist wing. If the BJP hardliners were to gain the upper hand, the party could adopt a much tougher stance toward Pakistan.

❖ The current negotiating is a bilateral affair, and there is only limited scope for active external engagement. Of foreign countries, China could possibly become a more significant factor. China has long, intimate ties with Pakistan and has been improving relations with India. If Beijing and New Delhi were to succeed in resolving their long-standing border dispute, China would be in a position to play a larger, behind-the-scenes role if it chose to do so.

❖ Should a new India-Pakistan crisis develop, a possibility given past history, the United States and the European Union will surely resume attempts to dampen tensions in order to avert possible conflict. For its part, the United States seems disinclined to alter its approach of recent years, active engagement during times of high tension and less visible behind-the-scenes encouragement during other times. The European Union lacks a sufficiently coherent diplomacy to do much more than urge the two sides on in their bilateral normalization efforts.

The history of peace process efforts, such as with Northern Ireland, Cyprus, Israel-Palestine, Sri Lanka, and other major disputes, makes clear that finding the solution is difficult and lengthy. Broad India-Pakistan reconciliation, including a Kashmir settlement, will surely require many years, perhaps decades, to achieve. Genuine normalization will involve tough, often painful negotiations, and difficult concessions by both Islamabad and New Delhi. Had the problems been easy, they would have been solved long ago. At least India and Pakistan have now initiated and sustained a comprehensive negotiating process for the past two years. If they can maintain this structured approach to normalizing relations, problems will gradually be resolved, differences will diminish, reciprocated confidence will grow, and mutual distrust will decline. If, however, the dialogue stalls, as it well may, then the history of India-Pakistan negotiating failures will once more repeat itself and past will remain prologue. As 2006 begins, the outlook is unclear.

Abridged Text of the Indus Waters Treaty

(Signed in Karachi on September 19, 1960)

The Government of India and the Government of Pakistan, being equally desirous of attaining the most complete and satisfactory utilisation of the waters of the Indus system of rivers and recognising the need, therefore, of fixing and delineating, in a spirit of goodwill and friendship, the rights and obligations of each in relation to the other concerning the use of these waters and of making provision for the settlement, in a cooperative spirit, of all such questions as may hereafter arise in regard to the interpretation or application of the provisions agreed upon herein, have resolved to conclude a Treaty in furtherance of these objectives, and for this purpose have named as their plenipotentiaries:

The Government of India: Shri Jawaharlal Nehru, Prime Minister of India, and The Government of Pakistan: Field Marshal Mohammed Ayub Khan, H.P., H.J., President of Pakistan, who, having communicated to each other their respective Full Powers and having found them in good and due form, have agreed upon the following Articles and Annexes.

ARTICLE II
PROVISIONS REGARDING EASTERN RIVERS

All the waters of the Eastern Rivers shall be available for the unrestricted use of India, except as otherwise expressly provided in this Article.

ARTICLE III
PROVISION REGARDING WESTERN RIVERS

Pakistan shall receive for unrestricted use all those waters of the Western Rivers which India is under obligation to let flow under the provisions of Paragraph (2). India shall be under an obligation to let flow all the waters of the Western Rivers, and shall not permit any interference with these waters, except for the following uses, restricted in the case of each of the rivers, The Indus, The Jhelum and The Chenab, to the drainage basin thereof: (a) Domestic Use; (b) Non-Consumptive Use; (c) Agricultural Use, as set out in Annexure C; and (d) Generation of hydro-electric power, as set out in Annexure D.

ARTICLE VIII
PERMANENT INDUS COMMISSION

India and Pakistan shall each create a permanent post of Commissioner for Indus Waters, and shall appoint to this post, as often as a vacancy occurs, a person who should ordinarily be a high-ranking engineer competent in the field of hydrology and water-use. Unless either Government should decide to take up any particular question directly with the other Government, each Commissioner will be the representative of his Government for all matters arising out of this Treaty, and will serve as the regular channel of communication on all matters relating to the implementation of the Treaty, and, in particular, with respect to (a) the furnishing or exchange of information or data provided for in the Treaty; and (b) the giving of any notice or response to any notice provided for in the Treaty.

The status of each Commissioner and his duties and responsibilities towards his Government will be determined by that Government. The two Commissioners shall together form the Permanent Indus Commission. The purpose and functions of the Commission shall be to establish and maintain co-operative arrangements for the implementation of this Treaty and to promote co-operation between the Parties in the development of the waters of the Rivers. The Commission shall determine its own procedures.

ARTICLE IX
SETTLEMENT OF DIFFERENCES AND DISPUTES

Any question which arises between the Parties concerning the interpretation or application of this Treaty or the existence of any fact which, if established, might constitute a breach of this treaty shall first be examined by the Commission, which will endeavor to resolve the question by agreement.

If the Commission does not reach agreement on any of the questions mentioned in the Paragraph (1), then a difference will be deemed to have arisen, which shall be dealt with by a Neutral Expert. If the Neutral Expert has informed the Commission that, in his opinion, the difference should be treated as a dispute, then a dispute will be deemed to have arisen.

As soon as a dispute to be settled has arisen, the Commission shall, at the request of either Commissioner, report the fact to the two Governments, as early as practicable, stating in its report the points on which the Commission is in agreement and the issues in dispute, the views of each Commissioner on these issues and his reasons therefore.

Either Government may, following receipt of the report, or if it comes to the conclusion that this report is being unduly delayed in the Commission, invite the other Government to resolve the dispute by agreement.

A court of Arbitration shall be established to resolve the dispute.

(The full text of the agreement can be found at the Henry L. Stimson Center website, www.stimson.org.)

Elements of a Kashmir Settlement

It is proposed that the following points, which are designed to encourage the parties to concentrate on the immediate questions at issue, should be put to the parties by the Ambassador and by Elmore Jackson after the latter's arrival on the subcontinent.[72] The British, through their High Commissioners, will concert, as appropriate, in the presentation and the subsequent discussion.

1. Neither India nor Pakistan can entirely give up its claim to the Kashmir Valley. Each must have a substantial position in the Vale.

2. India and Pakistan must both have assured access through the Vale for the defense of their positions to the north and east. These defense arrangements must be such as not to impede a disengagement of Indian and Pakistani forces.

3. Outside the Valley, the economic and strategic interests of the two countries should be recognized, e.g., India's position in Ladakh and Pakistan's interest in the development of water storage facilities on the Chenab.

4. The position of the two countries in the Valley must be such as to permit:

    (a) clearly defined arrangements for sovereignty and for the maintenance of law and order.

    (b) political freedom and some measure of local self-rule for the inhabitants.

    (c) free movement of the people of the Valley throughout the Vale and their relatively free movement to other parts of Kashmir and to India and Pakistan.

    (d) the rapid development by India and Pakistan of tourism in the Kashmir area—with its important foreign exchange potential for both countries.

(e) the effective use in Kashmir of development funds, available from external sources, for such purposes as improving water and forestry resources, the development of communications and small industries, and improving the health and welfare of the people.

Text from *Foreign Relations of the United States, 1961–1963, Vol. XIX*, 534, Attachment to Memorandum from Secretary of State Rusk to President Kennedy.

The Tashkent Declaration

The Prime Minister of India and the President of Pakistan having met at Tashkent and having discussed the existing relations between India and Pakistan hereby declare their firm resolve to restore normal relations between their countries of vital importance for the welfare of the 600 million people of India and Pakistan.

(i) The Prime Minister of India and the President of Pakistan agree that both sides will exert all efforts to create good neighbourly relations between India and Pakistan in accordance with the United Nations Charter. They reaffirm their obligation under the Charter not to have recourse to force and to settle their disputes through peaceful means. They considered that the interests of peace, particularly in the Indo-Pakistan subcontinent, and indeed, the interests of the peoples of India and Pakistan were not served by the continuance of tension between the two countries. It was against this background that Jammu & Kashmir was discussed, and each side set forth its respective position.

TROOPS WITHDRAWAL

(ii) The Prime Minister of India and the President of Pakistan have agreed that all armed personnel of the two countries shall be withdrawn not later than 25 February 1966 to the positions they held prior to 5 August 1965, and both sides shall observe the cease-fire terms on the cease-fire line.

(iii) The Prime Minister of India and the President of Pakistan agreed that relations between India and Pakistan shall be based on the principle of non-interference in the internal affairs of each other.

(iv) The Prime Minister of India and the President of Pakistan have agreed that both sides will discourage any propaganda directed against the other country and will encourage propaganda which promotes the development of friendly relations between the two countries.

(v) The Prime Minister of India and the President of Pakistan have agreed that the High Commissioner of India to Pakistan and Commissioner of Pakistan to India will return to their posts and that the normal functioning of diplomatic missions of both countries will be restored. Both Governments shall observe the Vienna Convention of 1961 on Diplomatic Intercourse.

TRADE RELATIONS

(vi) The Prime Minister of India and the President of Pakistan have agreed to consider measures towards the restoration of economic and trade relations, communications as well as cultural exchanges between India and Pakistan, and to take measures to implement the existing agreement between India and Pakistan.

(vii) The Prime Minister of India and the President of Pakistan have agreed that they will give instructions to their respective authorities to carry out the repatriation of the prisoners of war.

(viii) The Prime Minister of India and the President of Pakistan have agreed that the two sides will continue the discussions of questions relating to the problems of refugees and eviction of illegal immigrants. They also agreed that both sides will create conditions which will prevent the exodus of people. They further agree to discuss the return of the property and assets taken over by either side in connection with the conflict.

SOVIET LEADERS THANKED

(ix) The Prime Minister of India and the President of Pakistan have agreed that the two sides will continue meetings both at highest and at other levels of matters of direct concern to both countries. Both sides have recognized the need to [set] up joint Indian-Pakistani bodies which will report to their Governments in order to decide what further steps should be taken.

(x) The Prime Minister of India and the President of Pakistan record their feelings, deep appreciation and gratitude to the leaders of the Soviet Union, the Soviet Government and personally to the Chairman of the Council of Ministers of the USSR for their constructive, friendly and noble part in bringing about the present meeting which has resulted in mutually satisfactory results. They also express to the Government and friendly people of Uzbekistan their sincere thankfulness for their overwhelming reception and generous hospitality.

They invite the Chairman of the Council of Ministers of the USSR to witness this declaration.

Prime Minister of India
Lal Bahadur Shastri

President of Pakistan
Mohammed Ayub Khan

Tashkent, January 10, 1966

The Simla Agreement

The Government of India and the Government of Pakistan are resolved that the two countries put an end to the conflict and confrontation that have hitherto marred their relations and work for the promotion of a friendly and harmonious relationship and the establishment of durable peace in the sub-continent, so that both countries may henceforth devote their resources and energies to the pressing task of advancing the welfare of their peoples. In order to achieve this objective, the Government of India and the Government of Pakistan have agreed as follows:

(i) That the principles and purposes of the Charter of the United Nations shall govern the relations between the countries;

(ii) That the two countries are resolved to settle their differences by peaceful means through bilateral negotiations or by any other peaceful means mutually agreed upon between them. Pending the final settlement of any of the problems between the two countries, neither side shall unilaterally alter the situation and both shall prevent the organization, assistance or encouragement of any acts detrimental to the maintenance of peaceful and harmonious relations;

(iii) That the pre-requisite for reconciliation, good-neighbourliness and durable peace between them is a commitment by both countries to peaceful co-existence, respect for each other's territorial integrity and sovereignty and non-interference in each other's internal affairs, on the basis of equality and mutual benefit;

(iv) That the basic issues and causes of conflict which have bedeviled the relations between the two countries of the last twenty-five years shall be resolved by peaceful means;

(v)   That they shall always respect each other's national unity; territorial integrity; political independence and sovereign equality;

(vi) That in accordance with the Charter of the United Nations, they shall refrain from the threat or use of force against the territorial integrity or political independence of each other.

(II)   Both Governments will take all steps within their power to prevent hostile propaganda directed against each other.

Both countries will encourage the dissemination of such information as would promote the development of friendly relations between them.

(III) In order progressively to restore and normalize relations between the two countries step by step, it was agreed that:

(i)   Steps shall be taken to resume communications, postal, telegraphic, sea, land including border posts, and air links including overflights;

(ii)   Appropriate steps shall be taken to promote travel facilities for the nationals of the other country;

(iii) Trade and co-operation in economic and other agreed fields will be resumed as far as possible;

(iv)   Exchange in the fields of science and culture will be promoted.

In this connexion delegations from the two countries will meet from time to work out the necessary details.

(IV) In order to initiate the process of the establishment of durable peace, both Governments agree that:

(i)   Indian and Pakistani forces shall be withdrawn to their side of the international border;

(ii)   In Jammu and Kashmir, the Line of Control resulting from the cease-fire of December 17, 1971 shall be respected by both sides without prejudice to the recognized position of either side. Neither side shall seek to alter it unilaterally, irrespective of mutual differences and legal interpretations. Both sides further undertake to refrain from the threat of the use of force in violation of this line;

(iii) The withdrawals shall commence upon entry into force of this agreement and shall be completed within a period of thirty days thereof.

(V) This Agreement will be subject to ratification by both countries in accordance with their respective constitutional procedures, and will come into force with effect from the date on which the Instruments of Ratification are exchanged.

(VI) Both Governments agree that their respective Heads will meet again at a mutually convenient time in the future and that, in the meanwhile, the representative of the two sides will meet to discuss further the modalities and arrangements for the establishment of a durable peace and normalization of relations, including the questions of repatriation of prisoners of war and civilian internees, a final settlement of Jammu and Kashmir and the resumption of diplomatic relations.

Indira Gandhi	Zulfiqar Ali Bhutto
Prime Minister	President
Republic of India	Islamic Republic of Pakistan

The Lahore Declaration

The Prime Ministers of the Republic of India and the Islamic Republic of Pakistan:

Sharing a vision of peace and stability between their countries, and of progress and prosperity for their peoples;

Convinced that durable peace and development of harmonious relations and friendly cooperation will serve the vital interests of the peoples of the two countries, enabling them to devote their energies for a better future;

Recognising that the nuclear dimension of the security environment of the two countries adds to their responsibility for avoidance of conflict between the two countries;

Committed to the principles and purposes of the Charter of the United Nations, and the universally accepted principles of peaceful co-existence;

Reiterating the determination of both countries to implementing the Simla agreement in letter and spirit;

Committed to the objective of universal nuclear disarmament and non-proliferation;

Convinced of the importance of mutually agreed confidence building measures improving the security environment;

Recalling their agreement of 23rd September, 1998, that an environment of peace and security is in the supreme national interests of both sides and that the resolution of all outstanding issues, including Jammu and Kashmir, is essential for this purpose;

Have agreed that their respective Governments:

❖ shall intensify their efforts to resolve all issues, including the issue of Jammu and Kashmir.

❖ shall refrain from the intervention and interference in each other's internal affairs.

❖ shall intensify their composite and integrated dialogue process for an early and positive outcome of the agreed bilateral agenda.

❖ shall take immediate steps for reducing the risk of accidental or unauthorised use of nuclear weapons and discuss concepts and doctrines with a view to elaborating measures for confidence building in the nuclear and conventional fields, aimed at prevention of conflicts.

❖ reaffirm their commitment to the goals and objectives of SAARC and to concert their efforts towards the realisation of the SAARC vision for the year 2000 and beyond with a view to promoting the welfare of the peoples of South Asia and to improve their quality of life through accelerated economic growth, social progress and cultural development.

❖ reaffirm their condemnation of terrorism in all its forms and manifestations and their determination to combat this menace.

❖ shall promote and protect all human rights and fundamental freedoms.

Signed at Lahore on the 21st day of February 1999

Atal Behari Vajpayee   Muhammad Nawaz Sharif
Prime Minister of the   Prime Minister of the Islamic
Republic of India   Republic of Pakistan

NOTES

i. I am particularly appreciative of the thoughtful help and cogent advice offered by Paul Stares and Chris Fair of the United States Institute of Peace during various stages of this project. I am also grateful to Walter Andersen, K. Shankar Bajpai, Stephen Cohen, Robert Hathaway, William Milam, and Marvin Weinbaum who read the study in draft and offered numerous useful suggestions and corrections. Finally, I want to thank Dwijen Mehta and Valentina Pasquali, interns at the Woodrow Wilson Center who helped in numerous unglamorous, but invaluable ways in the research and preparation of the study.

1. The councils were consultative, not genuine law-making bodies. They lacked the power to introduce or block legislation, and the majority of members were still officially appointed.

2. See Stanley Wolpert, *Jinnah of Pakistan* (New York: Oxford University Press, 1984), 46–49, for a discussion of the era of Hindu-Muslim unity in which Jinnah played a key role.

3. Ibid., 69–72. In the late 1920s, Jinnah moved to London to practice law, and withdrew from an active role in Indian politics. He returned to India in 1934 when he assumed leadership of the Muslim League.

4. Ibid., 147–151. Wolpert describes the critical 1937 events that put Jinnah on the road to Pakistan.

5. Jinnah statement regarding the Lahore declaration, April 15, 1940, quoted in R.J. Moore, *Endgames of Empire: Studies of Britain's Indian Problem* (Delhi: Oxford University Press, 1988), 121.

6. This idea had been discussed earlier. In the 1920s, Veer Savarkar, the founder of the Hindu Mahasabha, the precursor to the Hindu nationalist RSS, spoke of two antagonistic nations living side-by-side in India.

7. Nehru statement quoted in Sir Penderel Moon, *The British Conquest and Dominion of India* (London: Duckworth, 1989), 1153.

8. Jinnah's July 29, 1946, statement quoted in Wolpert, *Jinnah of Pakistan*, 282–283.

9. Memorandum of President Johnson's meeting with President Ayub Khan, 4:30–5:30 P.M., December 15, 1965, Howard Wriggins files, India-Pakistan Military Assistance, Lyndon B. Johnson Library, Austin, Texas.

10. Thomas P. Thornton, "Pakistan: Fifty Years of Insecurity," *India and Pakistan: The First Fifty Years* (Washington, DC: Woodrow Wilson Center Press, 1999), 179.

11. See Dennis Kux, *India and the United States, Estranged Democracies, 1941–1991* (Washington, DC: National Defense University Press, 1992), 61, 62, 130, and 142 for accounts of Nehru's talks with U.S. leaders.

12. Obviously alternative approaches to the one employed in this study could possibly have suggested different outcomes.

13. The following sources refer to the conflict as the 1971 War: Brigadier Jagdev Singh, *Dismemberment of Pakistan: 1971 Indo Pak War,* (New Delhi: Lancer International, 1988); Major General Hakeem Arshad Qureshi, *The 1971 Indo-Pak War: A Soldier's Narrative* (Karachi: Oxford University Press, 2002); and Richard Sisson and Leo Rose, *War and Secession: Pakistan, India, and the Creation of Bangladesh* (Berkeley: University of California Press, 1990).

14. In Pakistan, the official title is the Ministry of Foreign Affairs while in India it is called the Ministry of External Affairs.

15. Text of Eisenhower September 9, 1960 statement, *Foreign Relations of the United States (FRUS), 1958–1960, Vol. XV,* 212.

16. W. Norman Brown, *The United States and India, Pakistan, and Bangladesh* (Cambridge: Harvard University Press, 1972), 165–166.

17. David Lilienthal, "Another Korea in the Making?" *Colliers,* v. 128 (August 4, 1951), 22–23.

18. An overview of the negotiations can be found in "The Indus Waters Treaty: A History," Henry L. Stimson Center, http://www.stimson.org/southasia.

19. Kux, *Estranged Democracies,* 150–151, and Sarvapelli Gopal, *Jawaharlal Nehru, Vol. 3, 1956–1964* (London: Oxford University Press, 1984), 133–138.

20. For greater detail, see Karachi Embassy telegram to State Department, May 19, 1959, *Foreign Relations of the United States, 1958–1960, Vol. XV,* 167–168; Memorandum of conversation on Indus Waters Negotiations, May 24, 1960, State Department Central Files, 690D.91322/4–2560, Department of State Records, National Archives, College Park, Maryland; Record of National Security Council meeting, May 28, 1959, *FRUS, 1958–1960, Vol. XV,* 7-8; Memorandum of conversation between Acting Secretary of State Douglas Dillon and President Eisenhower, November 8, 1959, *FRUS, 1958–1960, Vol. XV,* 178–182.

21. Kux, *The United States and Pakistan, 1947–2000: Disenchanted Allies* (Washington: Woodrow Wilson Center Press, 2001), 126.

22. John Kenneth Galbraith, *Ambassador's Journal: A Personal Account of the Kennedy Years* (Boston: Houghton Mifflin, 1969), 500.

23. Report of the Harriman Mission, 5–8, S/S Files, NSC Subcommittee on South Asia, DSR, NA and Record of the NSC Executive Committee meeting, December 3, 1962, *FRUS, 1961–1963, Vol. XIX,* 418.

24. Kux, *The United States and Pakistan,* 136–137.

25. Sir Morrice James, *Pakistan Chronicle* (New York: St. Martin's Press, 1993), 89–93. James was the British High Commissioner to Pakistan at the time.

26. James, *Pakistan Chronicle*, 94–96 and Embassy Karachi telegrams to the State Department, February 9–11, 1963, POL 32-1, India-Pak, DSR, NA.

27. Memorandum of conversation between Dean Rusk and Pakistani Ambassador Aziz Ahmed, February 23, 1963, *FRUS, 1961–1963, Vol. XIX*, 510.

28. Galbraith, *Ambassador's Journal*, 564–565.

29. "Kashmir: Tactics for Fifth Round," memorandum from Rusk to Kennedy, March 31, 1963, *FRUS, 1961–1963, Vol. XIX*, 529–534.

30. Komer memo to Kennedy, April 14, 1963, *FRUS, 1961–1963, Vol. XIX*, 553; Sarvepalli Gopal, *Jawaharlal Nehru, Vol. 3*, 259; and Embassy New Delhi telegram to the State Department, April 22, 1963, POL 32-1, India-Pak, DSR, NA.

31. Text of Kennedy's press conference in the *New York Times*, September 13, 1963.

32. For an account of the 1965 war, see Russell Brines, *The Indo-Pakistani Conflict* (London: Pall Mall P., 1968); Sir Morrice James, *Pakistan Chronicle*, 127–153, provide an insider's view by the former U.K. High Commissioner to Pakistan during the war.

33. Kux, *The United States and Pakistan*, 158–165.

34. *Washington Post*, December 9, 1965.

35. Kux, *The United States and Pakistan*, 166–168.

36. Altaf Gauhar, *Ayub Khan, Pakistan's First Military Ruler* (Lahore: Sang-e-Meel Publications, 1993), 379.

37. C.P. Srivastava, *Lal Bahadur Shastri: A Life in Politics* (New Delhi, 1995), 377–391.

38. See Srivastava, *L.B. Shastri*, 350–383 for an Indian insider's account of events at Tashkent and Altaf Gauhar, *Ayub Khan*, 377–391 for an account from Ayub's close advisor.

39. Altaf Gauhar, *Ayub Khan*, 393–399.

40. *Economist*, December 18, 1971, 11–12.

41. *Hindu*, June 26, 27, 28, 1972.

42. Articles in *Dawn* July 1 and 2, 1972, provide full accounts from the Pakistani perspective of the negotiations and the near breakdown over Kashmir, which Bhutto told the press was "the basic impediment."

43. *Dawn* and *Hindu*, July 3, 1972, provide full accounts of events from the Pakistani and Indian perspectives.

44. Interviews with Abdul Sattar, December 14, 1995, Islamabad, Pakistan, the late Ashok Chib, February 6, 2000, New Delhi, India, and Benazir Bhutto, October 12, 2003, Alexandria, Virginia. All were present at Simla.

45. *New York Times*, July 3, 1972.

46. Report of Connally visit to Pakistan is contained in a eight-part telegram sent from Embassy Tehran to Department of State, July 8, 1972, and obtained through a Freedom of Information Act request.

47. In a speech in New Delhi at the Hindustan Times Forum, December 12, 2003, Benazir Bhutto declared that her government had approved of what she called "low intensity warfare" to press the Indians on Kashmir. Her admission breached the official Pakistani position that Islamabad was giving moral and political but not materiel support to the Kashmir jihadis.

48. *New York Times*, February 21, 1999.

49. *Hindu*, February 22, 1999.

50. *News*, February 24, 1999.

51. *Washington Post*, February 24, 1999.

52. *Washington Post*, February 22, 1999.

53. *Hindu*, February 21, 1999.

54. Kux, *The United States and Pakistan*, 352–354.

55. Niaz Naik told the author that Vajpayee had urged him and Mishra to explore possible solutions. Niaz added that after checking with civilian and military leaders in Islamabad, he had tabled the same proposal that Pakistan had offered in the third round of the 1962–63 talks. Because of Kargil, the talks were aborted before the Indians responded. Although Mishra was unwilling to discuss any details of the back channel talks with the author, it is unlikely that the Pakistan offer would have provided a better basis for serious negotiations in 1999 than it had in 1963.

56. Sharif had made his own task more difficult by forcing Army chief Jehangir Karamat out of office and replacing him with General Pervez Musharraf. It seems unlikely that Karamat would have blessed the Kargil adventure.

57. *Dawn*, July 11, 14, 2001; *Hindustan Times*, July 18, 2001; and *New York Times*, July 14, 2001.

58. *New York Times*, July 15, 2001.

59. *Dawn*, July 16, 2001, and *Indian Express*, July 16, 2001.

60. *Hindustan Times*, July 19, 2001.

61. *New York Times*, July 17, 18, 2001 and *The Telegraph*, July 17, 2001.

62. *Hindustan Times*, July 18, 2001.

63. *Hindustan Times*, July 28, 2001.

64. Raymond Cohen, *Negotiating Across Cultures: Communication Obstacles in International Diplomacy*, rev. ed. (Washington, DC: United States Institute of Peace, 1997).

65. When, after leaving office, Secretary of State Colin Powell claimed that his intervention had helped conflict between India and Pakistan, former Foreign Minister Jaswant Singh publicly contradicted Powell.

66. Stephen P. Cohen, *The Idea of Pakistan* (Washington: Brookings Institution Press, 2004), 97–130.

67. Comment by top-level Pakistani official in conversation with the author, June 2003.

68. *Hindu*, February 18, 2004.

69. *Hindu*, February 18, 2005.

70. From the text of the Joint Statement issued at the conclusion of President Musharraf's visit to New Delhi. The statement was read by Prime Minister Manmohan Singh with Musharraf standing at his side, *Dawn*, April 19, 2005.

71. Verghese Koithara, *Crafting Peace in Kashmir* (New Delhi: Sage Publications, 2004), 290–292.

72. Jackson was a Washington-based State Department expert on Kashmir and had dealt with the issue in the United Nations context for a number of years.

About the Author

Ambassador Dennis Kux is a retired U.S. State Department South Asia specialist and a Senior Policy Scholar at the Woodrow Wilson Center in Washington, DC. He is the author of histories of U.S. relations with Pakistan and India and has written numerous articles and book chapters regarding South Asia. During his diplomatic career, Kux served three tours in India and Pakistan and was the India country director during the 1970s. He served as the Ambassador to the Ivory Coast from 1986 to 1989.